LESSONS LIFE HAS TAUGHT ME

LESSONS
LIFE HAS TAUGHT ME

JP VASWANI

First published 2015

ISBN 978-81-8328-385-4

Published by
Wisdom Tree
4779/23, Ansari Road
Darya Ganj, New Delhi-110 002
Ph.: 23247966/67/68
wisdomtreebooks@gmail.com

Printed in India

Contents

Foreword *vii*

1. You are Not Alone! 1
2. All is Well! 13
3. The Meaning of Surrender 21
4. Take Care of Your Thoughts 37
5. Not Stumbling Blocks, but Stepping Stones 47
6. Love One Another! 57
7. Where is God? 67
8. Closer, My God, to Thee! 75
9. Cure for the Heart 87
10. Convert Misfortunes into Blessings 95
11. Forgive and Forget 103
12. Worst Thing 111
13. The Past Does Not Bind Us 121

14. Miracles of God 129
15. Love is the Power 137
16. Give, Give, Give! 145
17. We Cannot Deceive Nature 153
18. Let Go, Let God! 159
19. Work or Love 167
20. Love is the Key 175
21. Purpose of Life 183
22. The Hidden Shakti 191
23. Words of Power 199
24. Enlightenment! 207
25. There is No Death 215
26. Free from Anger and Arrogance 223
27. Insults are Like Bad Coins 235
28. The Test of a Man 243
29. Why? 253
30. The Secret 263
31. Religion is Life 273

Foreword

Manush Janam durlabh hai
Hot na baran baar...

This human life is a great and rare blessing that God has bestowed upon us. Why is this so? Not because we Homo sapiens are gifted with intelligence; not because we can laugh and cry and think; not because this world offers its greatest pleasures to humans who are endowed with the capacity to experience joy and sorrow. No, not for any of these reasons do our saints claim that human life is a precious gift to us. Life is rare and precious to the thinking human being because it offers him the opportunity of liberation, attaining oneness with His Creator, and returning to the true homeland from whence he came!

However, that is not what everyone understands or accepts! On the contrary, people will tell you that life is meant to be savoured and enjoyed to the fullest extent. 'Carpe diem! Sieze the day!' calls out the ancient Roman writer. 'Rejoice while you are alive; enjoy the day; live life to the fullest; make the most of what you have. It is later than you think.'

What these people are trying to say is: Eat, drink and be merry, for tomorrow we die! But surely there's more to life than this?

I would rather go with the wise man who said, 'The purpose of life is life with purpose.' Life is what we make of it. And I firmly believe that life is the greatest school for us human beings—a school of management, life sciences, well-being, service, art, creativity, philosophy and people skills—all rolled into one! We come out of this school with flying colours when we have fulfilled the purpose for which God had sent us here. When I say 'school', I mean 'knowledge'. For school is not about textbooks and blackboards and vacations; a school is about learning, and at the end of every learning process, there are outcomes to be achieved and a 'passing out' to be attained. What would you and I like to do in this school is a choice that each one of us has to make. Shall we learn all the valuable lessons taught to us here and master the true essence of life? Or shall we spend a lifetime here, as people do at a coffee shop or bar; idling, waiting for time to pass us by? As I said, the choice is entirely ours.

I reiterate this: Life is God's greatest school, and our experiences are our best teachers. Therefore, I tell my friends, 'The day I do not learn something new is for me, a lost day!'

One important lesson I have imbibed is that life is not a pleasure hunting ground; each day that we spend here on this earth has become possible only due to the flawless handiwork of our Creator. If we do not make the most of this life, we will have to face our Maker as failures!

Sometimes we try to run away from unpleasant experiences, even as students run away from tests and tough assignments. But escape is not an option in life. We cannot avoid these experiences; even if we succeed in evading them temporarily, they will come back to us in a more formidable form, until we have learnt the lesson that they were meant to teach us in the first place. Therefore, let us not try to run away from experiences. So many experiences, which appear to be bitter, come to us to teach us lessons we need to learn. Suddenly, a dear one is snatched away from us by death. We suffer unexpected, and sometimes, huge losses in business. Without any warning symptoms, we fall ill. Out of the blue, a calamity strikes us; a misfortune befalls us. Instead of trying to run away from such experiences, let us move forward to greet every incident and accident, illness and adversity, with the words, 'Welcome friend, what lesson do you have to teach me?'

One of the earliest lessons I learnt was when I was a school student. I realised then that time was the most precious of all possessions. Time is our capital. Every minute, every moment is precious. There is an ancient proverb which says, 'A moment of time is like an ounce of gold, but you can't buy even a moment of time with any amount of gold.' We realise the value of the moment only when the last moment arrives. Alexander, the world conqueror, was defeated by a tiny insect. It is said that he died of malarial fever from a mosquito bite. As he lay dying in his white tent, the great conqueror asked, 'Is there anyone who will give me a healthy breath of his life? In exchange, I will give him my whole empire.' He got silence. Alexander exclaimed, 'I wasted all my breath, millions and millions of it, in carving out an empire, in exchange of which, I cannot get even a single breath!'

The river of time flows on. The hours quickly change into days, the days into months and the months into years. Suddenly, one day, the bell tolls for us and the call goes forth, 'Vacate the house—of the body!' The body drops down, and man realises, too late, that he has lost the golden opportunity of human birth; has thrown away his precious life without ever really coming to terms with its true nature and purpose. 'If life was meant to be a joke, I'm sorry, I haven't got it!' exclaimed a great comedian. He did not realise that life is actually not meant to be a joke. We must be as conscious, sensitive and particular about our time as we are with our money. We must use time creatively and never forget that every moment is just the right time to do a right thing. If we wait for more opportune moments, we may have to wait till eternity. Take care of your moments, I say to my friends, and the years will take care of themselves.

'Life is half spent before we even know it,' says poet George Herbert.

Therefore, there is a sense of urgency in discovering the purpose for which God sent us here, and fulfilling that purpose in the best way we can. In other words, we must fix a goal. So many of us, alas, are just moving, ambling along life's highway, without even being aware of where we are going. Time is neutral. It could be used either constructively or destructively. Therefore, let us fix a goal—secular or spiritual—and each day, strive to draw closer to that goal.

Let me tell you, I was privileged to be taught this lesson very early in my life. Fortunately for me, I felt drawn to my beloved and mentor at a comparatively early age. I was just a college student, and Sadhu Vaswani drew me like a magnet. At his feet, I learnt the supreme lesson that life and all its bounties are given to us as a loan only to be passed on to those whose need is greater than ours. We are here to help each other. The day I have not helped the needy—a brother here, a sister there, a bird here, an animal there, is a lost day indeed.

Sadhu Vaswani was a prophet of the revolution that is coming—the revolution of love. He revealed to us our kinship with all who suffer, our partnership with those in pain. You are not apart from others, he said; you and others are parts of the one whole. He lived in this vision of unity.

One day, Sadhu Vaswani went to a village. The village folk looked at his large, luminous, love-filled eyes and wondered who he was. 'Are you a Hindu or a Muslim?' they asked. And he answered, 'I know not who I am.' 'Do you believe in the mosque or in the temple?' they then probed. 'I know not,' he said. 'I only know that I and my brother are one. Children of the One God are we all. And this, too, I know, that salvation is neither in Kashi nor in Mecca. Whether you go to the Ganga or to the Jamuna, you carry heavy fetters on your feet, if you have not love in your hearts.'

The way of love is the 'little way'. It is the way of the little ones, the way which simple folk, such as we are, can tread. It is the way of bhakti—devotion, and surrender to the Lord. It is the way of longing, deep yearning for the soul's Beloved. As a miser longs for gold, as a lover longs for his beloved, as a child longs for its mother, even so, Sri Ramakrishna Paramahansa urges us, must you long for the Lord. The longing of the heart may break forth in tears. And as Sant Tukaram exclaims, 'Blessed are they who have tears in their eyes. The tears of bhakti are more precious than the holy waters of the Ganga, Jamuna and Godavari.'

With tearful eyes, the bhakta utters the cry of separation, 'O Lord, where art Thou? I have sought Thee, birth after birth, but have not yet been blessed with a glimpse of Thy beauteous Face. Have mercy on me, Lord, and reveal Thyself to me!'

In silence, the bhakta sits everyday, and in the agony of separation, cries out for love. Rising from his solitude, as he looks around him, he finds that the world is sad, broken, torn with tragedy and full of suffering. Such a world needs sympathy, compassion and love. So as the bhakta moves amongst men, he gives the service of love to all—the virtuous and the wicked alike. For all are the images of the One Lord of love, and love must be denied to none.

It is neither the will-to-power nor the will-to-live, but the will-to-become an instrument of God's help and healing, in this world of suffering and pain, that will lead to the fulfillment of man's divine destiny.

Love must flow out from us, not only to our fellow human beings, but also to every creature that has the breath of life. For the whole world is hungry for love. Every ant and insect, every dog, goat and lamb, every cow, horse and pig, every tiny chicken that is strangled, yearns for love. Love quickens the evolution of him who loves, and of him who is loved. Therefore, kill not creatures, nor eat their flesh, but give them the pure, unselfish love of your hearts, and you will be blessed and they will be blessed.

We need to grow in the spirit of reverence for all life. All life must be regarded as sacred. There can be no peace on earth until all killing stops, for the simple reason that if a man kills an animal for food, he will not hesitate in killing a human being whom he regards as an enemy.

I have studied the different religions of the world and the teachings of their great founders, and I have found that there is but one light in all religions. To study different religions in the spirit of sympathy and understanding is to know that each one of them emphasises the same fundamental truths. Fights and feuds and quarrels in the name of religion are meaningless. Nor do I believe in converting a man from one religion to another. All we need to do is help a Hindu become a true Hindu, a Muslim become a true Muslim, a Christian become a true Christian and so on. Are we not all children of the One Heavenly Father, the One Divine Mother of the universe?

Today, India seems to be passing through a difficult period of her history. I regard it as a transitional phase. I believe that the spirit of India is strong. It will in due course, assert itself. India has a mission to fulfil in the coming days. She has a message to give to the nations of the East and to the nations of the West—the message that there can be no true freedom without spirituality.

As I have moved on the pathways of life, the Lord, in His mercy, has brought me in touch with many enlightened souls. I spent the early years of my life in Sind, the land of my birth. I regard its soil as sacred. It was there that I first came in contact with a number of dervishes and fakirs, and later when I came to India, I was equally privileged to meet several saints and holy men here. From them I have learnt innumerable lessons. If I were to enumerate them all, they would fill volumes. I will but refer to a few of them:

1. In the endless adventure of existence, God and man are comrades. God is our one unfailing companion. He will never leave us. We may try to run away from Him. But He will continue to follow us as our own shadow. In the words of Edward Thompson, 'He is the "Heavenly Hound".'

2. There is a meaning of mercy in *everything* that happens to us. For God is all-love. He is all-wisdom. He is too loving to punish, too wise to make a mistake. Whatever happens in the Divine Providence happens for our good. Nothing happens a moment too early or too late. God's clocks are never too slow. Everything happens at the right time, to the right person, at the right place. Therefore, wherever God takes us, let us go; wherever He keeps us, let us remain. Let us never forget that all is well, all was well, all will be well, both today and a hundred years hence.

3. When man surrenders himself to God, He takes upon Himself his entire responsibility. All we need to do is to hand ourselves over, with childlike trust, to the Lord. And the Angels of God will go ahead of us to clear the way. We shall be free from fear, anxiety, worry, stress and tension. We shall find that all our needs are provided for even before we become aware of them.

4. Thought is a tremendous force in the life of every individual. Thoughts shape our attitudes. Attitudes mould our character. Character influences our life. By changing our thought pattern, we can change our life.

5. Problems and challenges are not a dead end; they are only a bend in the road. Problems are not stumbling blocks; they are stepping stones to a better, richer and more radiant life. Often, problems become the door through which God enters our lives. We have surrounded ourselves with hard shells that keep God away. Problems crack the shells and God easily enters our lives.

6. Neither rites nor rituals, neither creed nor ceremonies are needed to improve the condition of the world. All that is needed is love for one another.

7. Are you anxious to find God? Then you must be prepared to lose yourself! Do you want God to be yours? Then you must first become His!

8. How may we know that we are drawing closer to God? The closer we draw to God, the more tender and compassionate become our hearts to the needs of those around us.

9. What is the best exercise for the heart? Reach down and lift up as many as you can.

10. Misfortunes are blessings if we handle them well. They are like knives, which hurt or help, depending how we hold them, by the blade or handle.

11. Life is too short to be spent in fault-finding, holding grudges or keeping memory of wrongs done to us. Forgive even before forgiveness is asked for. Forgive and forget.

12. The worst thing that can happen to a man is that he has a hot head and a cold heart.

13. If a person has moved in the wrong direction, he can always make a U-turn. The Angels of God will be with him. The past does not, and cannot bind us!

14. You, who are looking for miracles, open your eyes and see! All around us are the miracles of God. A tiny seed grows into a huge banyan tree. A caterpillar becomes a butterfly.

15. Open thine heart and let love enter in, and all things in the universe will gravitate to thee. For love is the power that pulls.

16. Give, give, give—until it hurts to give! This will release you from bondage to the ego, and to things.

17. I must never forget that every thought I think, every word I utter, every action I perform, every feeling, every emotion that wakes up within me, is recorded in the memory of nature. I may be able to deceive those around me; I may even succeed in deceiving myself, but I cannot deceive nature.

18. When a particular problem has vexed you for sometime, and you

are unable to do anything about it, hand it over to God. Breathe out the aspiration, 'Thy Will be done, O Lord!' Soon a way will be shown to you.

19. Does God want our work? Or does He want our love? He wants that we should work for Him in love.

20. If you wish to know God and understand Him, you must love Him more and more. The more you love Him, the more you will know Him. The key to knowledge is love!

21. The aim of life is to realise that we are immortal spirits, not the bodies we wear.

22. An infinite potential lies hidden within us. We are unaware of it, because we think of ourselves as limited, restricted creatures. We have identified ourselves with a biochemical mental organism. Our true self is the Atman. *Tat twam asi!* That art thou! There can be no limit to what we can do and achieve!

23. When all around us the storms blow and the tempests roar, let us close our eyes, think of God and repeat the words, 'God is with me, and He is in control.' These are words of power and can quell the fiercest storm.

24. No man can attain enlightenment just with his own efforts. Enlightenment cometh to man by the Grace of God. Strive for enlightenment—yes. But be like the peasant who tills the soil and sows the seed, then turns to the heavens for *chandi ka gola*—the silver drops of rain.

25. The greatest illusion from which man suffers is perhaps the illusion of death. In reality, there is no death. Death is very much like the sunset. When the sun sets here, it has already risen elsewhere. Likewise, death here is birth elsewhere. For life is eternal.

26. The greatest intoxication is that of the ego. The worst madness is

that of anger. The person who is free from arrogance and anger, finds goodness and beauty wherever he goes.

27. Has someone offended or insulted you? Insults are like bad coins. You cannot avoid them, but you can always refuse to accept them.

28. The test of a man is: How much he can bear, and how much he can share and how soon he confesses a mistake and makes amends for it.

29. If while praying, we can think of worldly matters, why can we not, while doing worldly things, think of God?

30. Think positively. Eat sparingly. Exercise regularly. Walk as much as you can. Be careful to see that your thoughts and actions are clean. A guilty mind breeds many diseases. Herein, lies the secret of a happy, healthy and harmonious life.

31. I have met many who will go to any lengths to prove the superiority of their religion over those of others. They will hold endless discussions and debates. They will even fight for it, and die for it. But I have met very few who live for their religion—who bear witness to the great teachings in deeds of daily living. Religion is life!

The above lessons are not personal truths which I set out to discover on my own; they are universally valid and relevant lessons that have been reiterated again and again by great sages and thinkers of the East and West. I have but distilled the essence of their wisdom, and tried in my own humble way, to translate them into deeds of daily living. I feel privileged to share them with you through the pages of this book.

—JP Vaswani

Lesson 1

YOU ARE NOT ALONE!

In the endless adventure of existence, God and man are comrades. God is our one, unfailing companion. He will never leave us. We may try to run away from Him. But He will always stay with us like our shadow. In the words of Edward Thompson, 'He is the "Heavenly Hound".'

He who prays to the Lord, and leans only on the Lord for support, is ever free from fear and worry. To fulfil our wishes, we too look for support and guidance, but we tend to depend more on worldly forces. Alas, all material things are subject to decay and destruction. Physical forms or objects are generally ephemeral. The Lord is the only eternal and permanent being, the one who is always with us. All we need to do is forge a close and loving relationship with Him—make Him our Mother, our Father and even our Master, if we so wish. Bond with Him the way our heart prefers, and we will never lose our way in the journey of life.

There is an ancient legend about a little boy called Gopal. He lived with his widowed mother in a broken-down hut, perched on the outskirts of a small village, adjoining a jungle. Everyday, he had to walk through the jungle to reach school. In the mornings, when the sun shone brightly and the jungle seemed unthreatening, the boy enjoyed the walk. But, when he returned from school at dusk, it was a completely different story. Darkness hung about like a shroud around the treetops. The boy jumped even at shadows and shook in terror every time a wild creature howled or roared to break the stillness of the jungle. Walking back home in the dark became an ordeal.

Finally, one day, consumed by fear, little Gopal announced to his mother, 'I won't go to school any more.'

'But why, my dear child?' asked the mother, perturbed. 'What made you say this today?'

'You don't know mother, how terrified I get every evening on my way back,' let out Gopal. 'I can't cross that jungle in the dark anymore.'

'But why should you be afraid?' pronounced his mother. 'Didn't you know your elder brother lives in the forest? You only have to call out to Him, and He will come and take you by the hand and lead you home safely.'

'Really?' It was the first time the boy had heard of this brother, so he was a bit skeptical. 'Do I actually have an elder brother who dwells in the forest? What is his name?'

'His name is Krishna,' the mother then revealed. 'Now, whenever you feel afraid, just call out, Krishna! Krishna! and He will be with you instantly.'

Gopal did not think of his brother when he walked to school the next morning. But when a wild cry pierced the jungle on his way back home, chilling him to the bone, his mother's words came all rushing back to him. Reining in his fear, Gopal then called out to his brother, 'Krishna! Krishna!' It was a loud cry from an innocent heart.

And Sri Krishna immediately responded. Appearing before the boy that instant with a flute on His Lips, He smiled at the little boy and said, 'Tell Me, My dear brother, what can I do for you?'

'I am all alone,' complained Gopal. 'Night is falling, and these strange noises in the jungle terrify me.'

'Be not afraid, my brother,' Sri Krishna said to the little boy. 'I am with you,' He reassured. 'I shall take you by the hand and see that you reach home safely.'

And so it came to be every evening. Gopal would call out to his 'brother', and Sri Krishna appeared without fail to lead him through the dark forest.

Days passed. Gopal began crossing the jungle without fear, attending school regularly. One day, his guru announced that his daughter's wedding would be celebrated the following day. He then invited all the boys to the wedding, asking them to come and enjoy the feast. Happy and excited, the boys couldn't stop talking about the wedding. They decided to carry a gift each for their guru's daughter.

That evening, Gopal asked his mother, 'Will you give me something to gift my guru's daughter? We have all been invited to her wedding.'

The mother nodded her head sadly. 'I wish I could. But my child, I have nothing to give you.'

Gopal was distressed. How could he go to the wedding empty-handed? What would the other boys say? What would the guru think of him?

The next morning, as he crossed the jungle, Gopal called out to his brother. It was the first time that he had sought him out in the morning.

'Krishna! Krishna!' he cried out.

The Lord appeared before him instantly. Little Gopal looked up at Him and pleaded, 'My dear brother, can you please give me a gift to take for my guru's daughter? Today is her wedding day, and we have all been invited to the feast.'

Sri Krishna then gave him a small bowl filled with milk. 'Take this with you,' He said with a smile. 'Offer this gift to the bride.'

Gopal took the bowl and set off. A shade of embarrassment lurked in his heart. For it was such a humble gift. But then, thought Gopal, it was better than going empty-handed!

Arriving at the wedding, a shy and hesitant Gopal offered the tiny bowl of milk to his guru. His teacher accepted the bowl but kept it in a corner, not paying much attention to the gift or the giver. Gopal felt ashamed. His gift seemed quite insignificant when compared to the interesting and expensive things other boys had brought. As each boy walked past Gopal's bowl to hand over his gift to the guru, the bowl got accidentally knocked over, again and again. Every time some milk was spilled out, and eventually it got empty.

Gopal was upset. Humble though it was, I did bring a gift for the bride, he thought. But it's of no use to anyone now as all the milk has been spilt.

The empty bowl then rolled over to the guru's feet. He picked it up and straightened it. And before his astonished eyes, the bowl filled up again with milk.

The guru scratched his head and wondered, 'What is this that I see? All the milk in the bowl was spilt just a moment ago. How can the bowl be full once again?'

He called out to his wife, 'Bring me a large vessel.'

She brought the biggest one. The bowl of milk was emptied into the vessel. But instantly, it stood full to the brim once again. Though the guru kept pouring out milk into the vessel, the little bowl filled up again and yet again with milk. The huge vessel threatened to overflow, but the little bowl was not empty.

This is no ordinary bowl, the guru said to himself. It is magical. There is definitely some miraculous power in it. Yet, it had seemed such an ordinary gift, he reflected, and chided himself for hardly noticing it before.

Turning to Gopal, the guru questioned, 'Tell me my child, where did you get this bowl?'

Gopal was equally amazed. 'Guruji,' he replied, 'my elder brother who dwells in the jungle gave me this bowl so that I could offer it to you as a gift. I was so ashamed to bring such a humble gift. I had no idea, it was a magic bowl.'

'Your brother who lives in the jungle?' frowned the master. 'Pray tell me his name.'

'Krishna,' Gopal revealed with pride.

'Krishna!' repeated the master, in disbelief. 'Tell me more about your brother, Gopal. What does he look like, what does he do?'

His eyes shining, Gopal replied, 'Every evening, as I cross the jungle, I call out to him. And he comes out of nowhere, with a flute on his lips and walks home with me. He plays the most beautiful melody on his flute, it touches my very heart, every time.'

'He appears out of nowhere, with a flute on his lips!' repeated the guru, dazed. 'And you say his name is Krishna!'

His daughter and her wedding forgotten, the guru now knelt before Gopal and implored to him, 'Please take me to see your brother. I too long to meet him.'

'Gladly will I take you to him,' agreed the innocent Gopal, and the guru and pupil set out for the jungle. The students, the guests and even the bride and groom followed behind, in a trance. Gopal's story and his miraculous gift had left them all awestruck.

Walking into the forest, Gopal called out, 'Krishna! Krishna! Where are you?'

But the Lord did not appear.

Gopal began to cry. 'Krishna!' he called out again. 'Krishna! Where are you? Why don't you come to me as you do everyday? My guru and all these people will think I am a liar! You must save me, and show these people that I spoke the truth about You. It is for you to save my good name!'

And then, they all heard this voice, 'My dear brother, your guru and all the people with you cannot see Me for their hearts are not pure and innocent as yours. Let them first cleanse their minds and hearts, and then come to Me. Then will they behold Me, as you have done!'

The guru turned to Gopal with tear-filled eyes. 'Blessed are you, my child!' he cried. 'The Lord has spoken the truth, for our hearts are indeed darkened by selfishness and passion. Little did I appreciate the value of your precious gift, for I only considered its worldly value.'

Dear friends, this wide world is a kind of jungle too, where often we are haunted by fearful shadows and unseen forces. Overcome with worry and dread, we may begin to despair about our fate. The more we think about it, the blacker does the picture appear, and the weaker we feel to deal with it.

At such times, let us call out, as little Gopal did, 'Krishna! Krishna!' For when we call out to Him from the depths of our being, He will be with us in an instant, and we too will begin to witness a miraculous transformation in our lives.

Understanding

When you wake up every morning, say this prayer in the silence of your heart, 'I want God to grant me a special gift, a valuable blessing: The great gift of faith! I pray to God that my faith may always remain solid as a rock, unshaken, unmoved by the vicissitudes of life, and the ups and downs of fickle fortune.'

A man may be so affluent that he possesses enough material wealth to provide for his future generations; he may be at such heights of power that he enjoys unquestioned authority. But, let me tell you, if he lacks faith, his wealth and power amount to nothing. You can compare him to the poorest of the poor. For the poverty of spirit afflicts him! On the other hand, a man who barely possesses anything, has no great power, is perhaps richer. He may not be wealthy, but if he has faith in God, then he is a master of himself; he is a king, who wants nothing. A man of faith can live in stability and equanimity.

Warming Up

Have you or your friends ever made statements such as these:

'Well, I go to the temple or church, but I wouldn't describe God as my best friend.'

'I want to feel closer to God, but I'm not sure how to get there.'

Can you hear yourself in these statements? Do you know others who perhaps do? If so, try this:

For one day, carry God in your heart, take Him with you wherever you go. Involve Him in your day's activities. Talk to Him when you feel afraid, depressed or lonely. Seek His help when you feel lost or scared. Keep turning to Him for every little advice you need. If someone hurts you, tell Him about it and seek His comfort. At night, thank Him for being with you throughout the day. As you retire to bed at the end of the day, you will surely feel you have drawn closer to God.

Words of Wisdom

I will never leave you nor forsake you.

—Hebrews 13:5 (Old Testament)

The Lord is my shepherd; I shall not be in want.
He makes me lie down in green pastures.
He leads me beside quiet waters.
He restores my soul.

—Psalm 23

When I walk by the wayside, He is along with me. When I enter into company amid all my forgetfulness of Him, He never forgets me. In the silent watches of the night, when my eyelids are closed and my spirit has sunk into unconsciousness, the observant eye of Him who never slumbers is upon me.

—Thomas Chalmers

Lesson 2

All is Well!

Mercy underlines all that happens to us. For God is all-love. He is all-wisdom. He is too loving to punish, too wise to make a mistake. Whatever happens in the Divine Providence happens for our good. Nothing happens a moment too early or too late. God's clocks are never too slow. Everything happens at the right time to the right person at the right place. Therefore, wherever God takes us, let us go; wherever He keeps us, let us remain. Let us never forget that all is well, all was well and all will be well, both today and a hundred years hence.

There is an old Hebrew story about a poor rabbi named Eizik who lived in Krakow. One night, he dreamt that an angel was asking him to look for buried treasure under a bridge that led to the king's palace in Prague. Thrice, he had the same dream. Finally, the third time, Rabbi Eizik set out for Prague, determined to find the treasure.

Upon arrival, he found to his dismay, the bridge was closely guarded by soldiers, day and night. No way could he secretly dig for the treasure. The soldiers would nab and jail him immediately.

So he waited near the bridge, forlorn, marching near it, from sunrise to sundown. When night fell, the captain of the guards came up to him and enquired kindly, 'What is bothering you my friend? Can I be of any help to you at all?'

The captain's kindness emboldened Rabbi Eizik into revealing his mission. He blurted out the whole story of his dream, which had brought him all the way from Krakow to Prague.

Hearing all this, the captain laughed aloud, but not unsympathetically. 'So, my friend,' he said, 'to follow your dream, you have worn out all that shoe leather and come all the way to Prague. Why, if I had so much faith in my dreams, I would have gone to Krakow to look for the buried treasure under the kitchen stove of a Jew named Rabbi Eizik. Wouldn't I have been a fool?' Rabbi Eizik thanked the man for his kindness and travelled back home. He now started digging for the treasure under his own kitchen stove. And sure enough, he found it all lying there!

With this money, he built a house of worship, where he thanked the Lord everyday for helping him understand that his treasure was not out there in some distant place, but where he himself was.

Marcel Proust, the distinguished French writer, tells us, 'The real voyage of discovery consists not in seeking new landscapes, but in having new eyes.' Many of us hunger for something far away and yet-to-be, while everything we need actually resides within us!

Understanding

Walk with God today and trust Him for tomorrow! This priceless secret can help you attain true peace and lasting joy. Let the twin powers, 'faith' and 'trust', banish worry from your life. This is not blind faith that I'm talking about—it is strong, reasoned, well-founded faith in God's goodness and care. It is the positive power that enables you to stand up and fight, and overcome your problems successfully. Remember, I said, 'Walk with God,' not 'sit back and wait for God to do something!'

Lazy people do *not* deserve God's help! But if you put in your best efforts and leave the rest to the Lord, I'm sure He will fulfil His part of the deal.

When you place your trust in the Lord, when you surrender utterly and completely to His Divine Will, you will find wonderful things happening in your life!

Warming Up

Hum to yourself the following lines several times (To the tune of 'If You're Happy and You Know It').

If you're happy and you know it, thank the Lord (Sing two times).

If you're gloomy and you know it, thank the Lord (Sing two times).

If you're healthy and you know it, thank the Lord (Sing two times).

If you're ailing and you know it, thank the Lord (Sing two times).

If you're trusting and you know it, then your heart will surely show it.

If you're trusting and you know it, thank the Lord.

There must have been moments in your life when your mind rebelled against prevailing situations! But as time passed, in retrospect, you may find, the same situations might have led to new openings and revelations or may have eventually made you stronger. Make a list of these occasions and thank God for each one of them.

All glory to God!

Words of Wisdom

Give up everything to Him, resign yourself to Him and there will be no trouble for you. Then you will come to know that everything is done by His Will.

—*Sri Ramakrishna*

Trust in the lord with all your heart, and lean not upon your own understanding. In all your ways acknowledge Him, and He shall direct your path.

—*Proverbs 3:5-6*

He who has faith has... an inward reservoir of courage, hope, confidence, calmness and assuring trust that all will come out well—even though to the world it may appear to come out most badly.

—*BC Forbes*

Lesson 3

The Meaning of Surrender

When man surrenders himself to God, the Divine takes upon Himself the entire responsibility. All we need to do is hand ourselves over in childlike trust to the Lord. The Angels of God shall then walk ahead of us to clear the way. This will free us from fear, anxiety, stress, tension and all negative emotions. We will discover to our amazement that all our needs are provided for even before we become aware of them.

Paltu was the son of a poor bricklayer, who lived in a remote village near Jaisalmer, at the farthest western corner of India, bordering the desert. His family worked at a brick kiln, and Paltu's job was to carry the bricks from the kiln to the site where his father was employed, laying bricks for the humble cottages of the local populace. Their work involved walking long distances carrying loads of bricks, and so Paltu was not sent to school. You must remember that this story belongs to a time when life was not mechanised or automated as it is today. There were no trucks or tempos to ferry men and machine-made bricks along highways. Labour was cheap; men were available to do all heavy work manually, and that is how Paltu's family managed to eke out their living.

Every evening, when he returned from the brick kiln, Paltu would go to the village temple where Sri Krishna was the presiding deity. He would assist the village priest in cleaning the temple, fetch water for the pooja and generally run around doing whatever he was asked to do. As for the priest, he took a special liking to the sprightly young lad, who was quiet and very well-behaved. When it was time to lock up the temple and go home for the night, the priest would give him the bit of jaggery or banana, which had been the offering for the day. The two of them would shut, bolt and lock the temple door, after Paltu had taken several 'peeks' at the Lord to ensure that He was alright.

Early in the morning, Paltu would be back at the temple door, waiting for the priest to open the shrine. He would help in the temple until his father came to call out to him. At a very young age, Paltu became a Krishna bhakta; the priest took him under his wing and regaled him with stories from the Puranas and other scriptures.

Neither of them could actually recall when Lord Badrinath entered their conversation. Perhaps, Paltu was just seven years old at that time, when the priest mentioned the shrine of Badrikashram, where Lord Narayana is installed in His yogic posture, attracting thousands of devout pilgrims who hazard all the risks of inclement weather and mountainous terrain to worship at this remote shrine, which is considered to be the holiest amongst the famous *char dham* or four shrines of the Himalayas.

'Paltu, my dear lad, there is no place on earth like Badrikashram,' the priest said to the boy. 'It is an eternal city and Lord Narayana presides over it. I tell you, the mere sight of Badrikashram is enough to free a man from all the bondages of life. He is assured of liberation!' And he went on to tell Paltu about the sages Nara and Narayana who had performed their *tapasya* there, and obtained enlightenment directly from the Lord. He spoke of how the growing evil of the *kaliyuga* had actually driven the Lord away from Badrinath, with the ancient temple destroyed, and the sanctified *salagram* deity thrown out, until Adi Shankara rediscovered the deity submerged in the Narad Kund and had it reinstalled at the temple.

Paltu heard with rapt attention the *Bhagavad Purana* story, where Lord Krishna reveals to His friend and devotee, Uddhava, how in future He would be available only at the holy spot of Badrikashram—Badrinath. Lord Krishna gave Uddhava His sandals, asking him to carry them to Badrinath and place it there for people to worship. 'The slippers are still there for all to see,' said the priest. Paltu's face lit up when he heard this. The priest added with a smile, 'You are a devout and pious lad, Paltu! Do you know what our sacred Hindu scriptures say?' Paltu looked askance. The priest continued, 'Our scriptures proclaim that the life of a Hindu is incomplete without making a pilgrimage to Badrinath. When you grow up Paltu, you too must make it a point to visit Badrikashram.'

That very moment, at the tender age of seven, a desire to make that pilgrimage took root in Paltu's heart. Come what may, he pledged, one day, he will go to this holiest of holy shrines. Paltu knew not much of geography; all he gathered from the priest was that Badrinath was far, far away in the mountains, and the journey from Jaisalmer would be very long and arduous. 'But you will make it Paltu, if you are devout,' the priest added encouragingly. 'When I say you will make it, I don't mean you will manage it all on your own effort. The Lord will surely beckon you and bestow upon you His sacred darshan, if you truly and deeply desire it.'

The seed had been planted early in the mind of this simple and humble devotee of the Lord. As days passed, the boy's longing to visit Badrikashram and worship Lord Narayana in His yogic splendour only grew more ardent. Paltu wanted nothing more in life than to be blessed with the opportunity to worship at the holy shrine and seek liberation at the Feet of the Lord. He was convinced the Lord would definitely call him one day and give the promised darshan!

When the call finally did come, Paltu was seventy-five years old! Like our ancestors often say, 'There is a time and place for everything, and it is ordained by the Lord.' The time had come for Paltu to fulfil his childhood vow. True to his pledge, Paltu had kept aside his meagre savings solely for this purpose. Now drawing out all his worldly wealth, the seventy-five-year-old set out on the long and demanding journey.

In those days, there were no roads up the Garhwal hills to take pilgrims to Badrikashram. The rich would hire ponies or *dolis* carried by hefty men; the rest invariably had to trudge through over eighty miles of hilly terrain, pass crevices and rivers, even walk along narrow precipices to reach the shrine. The wealthy pilgrims were known to halt midway at special camps; eat food cooked by chefs hired just for these camps, then continue their journey after a refreshing break. As for Paltu, he ate the simple fare that some holy men dwelling in the small ashramas lining the route were charitable enough to offer. His eyes beheld the unspoilt charm and the natural beauty of the region, but at every turn, it was the splendour of the Lord's Divine Beauty that took his breath away! He was not like the modern tourists, who combine sightseeing with pilgrimage. Paltu hardly spoke to anyone; his lips kept chanting the name of Sriman Narayan instead. In his heart, glowed the image of the unseen deity, enshrined within since childhood.

Thus, it was that our grey-haired, rustic hero, in his torn and tattered clothes, walking barefoot and covered in the *kali kambal* given to him in charity, managed to ultimately reach Badrikashram one cold winter morning. He saw the temple nestled like a jewel amidst two lofty peaks, and he literally ran all the way to the steps of the temple. The words of the temple priest rang in his ears once again, echoing back from his childhood, 'There are many sacred pilgrimage spots in the heavens, earth and the nether world, but there has been none equal to Badri, nor shall there be.'

Paltu stood transfixed by the sight that greeted him. The temple priest, in his ceremonial robes was shutting the doors of the shrine, accompanied by chanting of mantras and the sounding of drums and pipes. Surrounding him, stood the villagers, all ready with bag and baggage to follow him. The chanting over, the party climbed down the temple steps and headed downhill, along the very path Paltu had just clambered up.

'What's happening?' Paltu asked a villager in wonder. 'Where is everyone off to?'

'Don't you know what time of the year it is?' replied the villager. 'Diwali is over and the temple is shutting down for winter. The priest locks the temple and goes down to Joshimath. The entire village leaves with him, and that's why we are all ready with our bag and baggage and cattle.'

'But…but…what about my darshan?' stammered Paltu, aghast at the sombre revelation. In all these years, no one had ever told him the Badrikashram temple shuts down for six months in the year from November to April. It hit him like a bolt out of the blue.

'My dear friend, it's not about you, no one can have darshan here during winter!' the villager tried to explain as kindly as he could. 'Why, in a few days from now, the entire village and the shrine will be covered in snow! No one can live here, and no one comes up the hills to worship during this time of the year. Why didn't you ask someone before you climbed up the hills? Surely your fellow travellers would have told you all this!'

But these past several days, Paltu had been travelling with his mind fixed on the darshan; he had barely spoken to anyone; he took almost no breaks to catch up with fellow pilgrims. He had single-mindedly been on a mission to fulfil his life's great vow, and it was this one thought that had filled his mind. He felt stupid, lost and defeated now. Tears rushed down from his eyes. In desperation, he fell at the feet of the head priest who led the procession.

'Panditji, Panditji,' he pleaded with all his heart. 'Please don't leave me adrift in my misery! I have come here at the end of my earthly journey, to catch just one glimpse of the Lord who dwells in my heart! All I want is that these eyes should behold Him but once before they close forever in death. Please do not go away without giving me the Lord's darshan!'

The head priest paused. He inspected Paltu from head to toe, and was not impressed by what he saw. Old, ragged, weak, poor, unshaven and unkempt. In the superior voice he reserved to address the poor devotees, the priest pronounced, 'My dear man, the doors of the shrine have been shut. It is a sacrilege to even think of opening them now. Go back home now and come in summer, when the snow starts melting, and you can have the Lord's darshan to your heart's content. I myself will arrange to provide you with food and accommodation at our dharamshala, and you can stay and have as many glimpses of Lord Badrinath as you wish. Now, stand aside and let us pass.'

But Paltu would not let go of the Pandit's feet. 'Sir, you see me, an old and decrepit man,' he wept. 'How can I go away and come back next summer? My days are numbered, and I have come here on the final pilgrimage of my life. I have walked for days on end, surviving on alms, to finally make it to the temple door. How can you shut the door on my face? Please open it for a minute, so that I may worship my Lord. I know for sure I will never be able to make it here again!'

The head priest was annoyed by this outburst, but the villagers were moved by plight of the poor old man. Incensed by this show of pity, the priest screamed, '*Murkha*! Are you ignorant and illiterate that you do not have respect for our traditions and customs? Don't you know, we humans must vacate Badrikashram in this season so that the devas and gods too can offer their prayers to the Lord in peace! Would you be so bold as to disturb the deva yajnas? I tell you, go away and do not propose such foolish things to me!'

Before Paltu could so much as raise his head from the ground, the priest had swept away with a swish of his heavy, silken robes. Paltu laid his head on the lowermost step of the temple and sobbed his heart out.

In just a few minutes, the temple town was empty. Only the swirling waters of the Alakananda River could be heard in the distance. Paltu did not move from his place. In his mind's eye, he saw the deity at Badrinath entwined with the familiar icon of the village temple. 'I need You and nothing but You,' he kept murmuring. 'I want You and nothing but You. I shall lie here and die here on Your steps, when death comes for me. So what if I am unable to have Your darshan? I have arrived at Badrikashram, and that is all You have given to me in my destiny. So be it. I shall die at Your doorstep, and reach You at the Eternal Abode which never ever closes its doors to the devout.'

Hours crept by and Paltu lay motionless, even as dusk began to fall.

And then, all of a sudden, he felt someone place a hand on his stooped shoulder. Paltu did not bother to look up. A kind and sweet voice then whispered in his ear, 'Baba, what are you doing here?'

Paltu then raised his head and made out the figure of a shepherd, silhouetted in the twilight. 'I came here to worship the Lord in Badrikashram,' he cried. 'But the Lord has willed otherwise. I am too old and tired to go back home now, and I intend to just spend my last days here, at His doorstep.'

'Night is falling, and it can get really cold out here in the open,' cautioned the kind stranger. 'Come with me, and I will take you to my dwelling place. You will at least be warm for the night and tomorrow, we can discuss what you want to do.'

A pair of strong hands helped Paltu get up. Next, he found himself being led away from the temple. He could sense that they were walking up the hill rather than downwards. The way was steep and rocky, and in the dark, he could not see clearly where they were headed. But he kept leaning heavily on the young man for support, holding on to his shepherd's crook. Surprisingly, Paltu felt light and free. A great weight of sorrow seemed to have gone from his shoulder, and he felt content to let the young man take him wherever he wanted.

Soon they arrived at the entrance to a cave in the mountains. The shepherd led him inside, and perched him on a heavy straw pallet strewn with soft grass. The cave was well-lit with an oil lamp that burnt brightly, in a corner. 'You must be hungry,' said the young man then, and brought out a little pot of honey and a dish of goat cheese. The two of them shared a cosy meal together, with Paltu telling the young man his life story, and the young man nodding his head knowingly and sympathetically. When the meal got over, Paltu felt quite happy and carefree.

'You must be really tired,' the young man remarked. 'Would you like to lie down?'

'On the other hand, I feel quite awake and cheerful now,' smiled Paltu. 'You are such a kind soul, and I don't know where all my sorrow and anxiety have fled since I have seen you! Let us sit up for a while and then I will go to sleep.'

'Just wait a minute,' said the young man. 'I will make arrangements for our entertainment.' He went out and returned with a few small, hard, black stones. With a piece of white limestone, he drew some crisscross lines on the floor of the cave and invited Paltu to come and sit before him on the floor. Placing the black stones on the crisscrossed lines, he taught Paltu the game of 'lambs and tigers', which they played with such relish that they failed to keep track of time. It was Paltu who first became aware of the sunlight creeping into the cave, and exclaimed, 'It's morning already!'

'Come Baba, I will take you to the hot springs here so that you may have a wash,' suggested the young man. Paltu allowed himself to be led again by the young man; he was however surprised to note that all the weariness coming from weeks and weeks of travel seemed to have magically disappeared from his limbs.

'You are a very kind young man,' praised Paltu gratefully as the duo walked down the hilly path. 'It has not been my good fortune to come across someone like you till now! But, as they say, better late than never! And, in my old age, I have learnt to value kindness far more than I did earlier.' Something hit Paltu then and he burst out, 'But, you haven't told me your name till now.'

'What else but Narayan?' let out his companion laughing. 'I belong here, and that's the name I was given.'

'Badrinarayan sent this Narayan to take care of me when I was heartbroken,' cried out Paltu, overwhelmed with gratitude. 'I simply cannot thank you enough for all the compassion you have shown me.'

Chatting thus, they reached the steps of the Tapt Kund—the hot water spring near the temple. Narayan led Paltu down the steps carefully, and helped him take the sacred dip. 'So what if He will not give me darshan!' pronounced Paltu with a calm and satisfied air as he immersed himself in the hot water, holding tightly onto Narayan's hand, 'I have had the ritual dip at Badrinath, and I have been treated with such kindness and affection by you.'

When they came out of the kund, Paltu said to Narayan, 'I will say a silent prayer now. And then I will return to the temple door and prostrate myself before Badrinathji one last time. And then I must be off from Badrikashram. I am so grateful to the Lord that He brought me here against all odds, and I am returning from this place, a peaceful and contented man, having met you.'

Narayan only smiled his benign smile, as he helped Paltu up the steps, and led him towards the temple. As they neared the place, the sound of chanting, drums, pipes and bugles reached their ears, and Paltu was taken aback to see a crowd before the temple, being led by the head priest. Unable to control his feelings, he burst out, 'O, Panditji, Panditji, you came back after all, for the sake of this old man! You came back to let me have one glimpse of my Badrinath before I left Badrikashram! And my brothers and sisters from the village have all come back to see this old man have his darshan! O, how kind you are, each and every one of you! I knew you were all kind people the moment I set eyes on you! And my Lord has sent you back here the very day after you left so that his old devotee should not return from here disappointed!'

The priest and the villagers stared wide-eyed at Paltu, neither believing nor comprehending what they saw and heard. Collecting himself finally, the priest asked in wonder, 'My man, how did you manage to survive here during the winter months? Where did you stay? What did you eat? And how is it that you look so blissful as if you are just stepping out of *swargaloka*?'

'But you left just yesterday,' repeated Paltu. 'As for me, I spent the night with my young friend in his shepherd's cave.' Turning around to point out his companion, and not seeing him there, Paltu called out, 'Narayan! Narayan, my dear Narayan, where are you?'

'Yesterday?' cried the priest. 'How can that be? We locked the temple up and left this place six months back!' Frowning at Paltu, he declared, 'Ask any of the villagers here, and they will tell you we are returning after six months! And you say, you spent the night in a shepherd's cave! Tell us, where is this shepherd you speak of?'

Paltu looked around, but Narayan was nowhere to be found. The villagers surrounded him then, and the temple priest clasped his hand, crying. 'Where is this Narayan?' he pleaded. 'Where is this young man who looked after you and protected you and kept you here in the snowbound mountains for six long months? What I would not give to see him with my eyes!'

Paltu stared at him amazed. Was it really six months since they had left? Was he in Narayan's cave for six long months? How did time fly so quickly? Was he in a different world, on a different plane? But, most important of all, where was Narayan?

The villagers were slowly catching on to what the priest was saying. The old man had managed to survive in the snowbound hills for six long winter months, and the most surprising thing was that he seemed to think it was just an overnight stay!

The temple priest took Paltu by the hand and led him up the steps. 'You are truly blessed!' he wept. 'We went away and Lord Badrinath looked after you Himself! Now, you will unlock the doors of the shrine and give us the darshan that we denied to you last year!'

Paltu was not a sharp man, but he understood what had happened. Nor was he surprised. For he knew that the Lord was Compassion Incarnate, and He had promised that it would be His business to look after His devotees, who surrendered to His Will, utterly and completely. Paltu was still looking around for his young friend, Narayan, although something told him that Narayan was not likely to present Himself now, among the milling crowd. 'When will I see Him again?' Paltu kept thinking even as the head priest thrust the massive key of the temple in his hand, and helped him turn the key in the lock. With all his might, Paltu pushed open the massive door, his mind still dwelling on Narayan. 'When will I see Him again? When will I see Him again?'

The doors opened. The *akhand jyot* lighted six months earlier was still shining brightly, and Paltu saw his Narayan, in the benign and sacred form of the deity in the sanctum sanctorum. The young shepherd seemed to smile at him. And behind him, the devotees chanted in unison, '*Jai Badrinathji ki!*'

UNDERSTANDING

Think of a difficult situation that you currently face in your life, one which you are unable to cope with. It could be an issue at work, a relationship problem with your near and dear ones, a financial or family situation or just something personal like trying to give up a bad habit like smoking.

Write down your problem on a piece of paper and put it in a box labelled 'For God'. Then go and get busy with some work. Forget about the problem. If your mind tries to think about the problem just repeat to yourself, 'It is God's problem now.' Soon you will find that God will show you a way out. He will guide you in some mysterious, unfathomable way, but the key is that you should have complete faith in Him, you should stop fretting and worrying and not try to 'take on' the problem yourself.

Warming Up

Today, sit down in silence for some time. Observe in detachment, every negative thought that passes through your mind. Label each one as you recognise it: 'Fear', 'Anxiety', 'Loss of Control', 'Stress', 'Anger' or 'Envy'. After watching the procession for some time, visualise these thoughts as being no more than paper labels, and imagine each one of them being carried away by a smiling angel with wings. Rejoice in the certainty that each one will be disposed off by a beautiful, loving angel of God!

Words of Wisdom

Abandoning all dharmas—rules and rituals,
take refuge in Me alone; I will liberate thee from
all sins; grieve not.

—*Srimad Bhagavad Gita*

Those who propitiate Me consistently desiring
to attain Me, with single-minded devotion—with
an undistracted mind, I take the responsibility
of their worldly as well as spiritual welfare.

—*Srimad Bhagavad Gita*

Surrender is faith that the power of love can
accomplish anything even when you cannot
foresee the outcome.

—*Deepak Chopra*

Lesson 4

Take Care of Your Thoughts

Thought is a tremendous force in the life of every individual. Thoughts shape our attitudes. Attitudes mould our character. Character determines our destiny. By changing our thought pattern, we can change our destiny.

The story of Dick Whittington and his cat is the subject of cartoons, fairy tales and pantomime shows, which are very popular with children. But, recent research has established that the character of Dick is in fact based on a real person. His story upholds the truth that if you change your thoughts, you can change your life.

As the story tells us, Dick was a poor lad from Gloucestershire, who dreamt of 'making it big'. He heard people talk of London, and they always described it as a city where a man could make or mar his fortune. The streets of London were paved with gold, they told him. And so, with stars in his eyes and dreams in his heart, Dick set out for London.

Alas, the reality of London was very different from the dream city he had conjured in his mind! London turned out to be a dirty, plague-infested city, where the pavements were not just filthy and strewn with garbage, but also crowded with the sick and dying poor. Finding it tough to survive in this inhospitable city, a starving Dick fainted outside the house of a merchant called Fitzwarren, who took pity on him and employed him as a servant.

Though Dick now had food to eat and a roof over his head, the basement of the Fitzwarren house where he slept with other servants was, to his dismay, infested with rats. But determined to stay on in the city which could make or mar his fortune, Dick bought a cat with the first salary he was given—the princely sum of one penny! The cat proved to be a boon for him and his fellow servants; it single-handedly put an end to all the rats in the basement, making life just a little more tolerable for Dick and his mates.

Dick continued to work hard for his master, whom he saw not only as a saviour but also as a role model. When Mr Fitzwarren bought his own ship for overseas trading, he invited his servants to send anything they themselves wished to offer on sale on board the ship, as it set out on its first voyage. Dick had nothing to offer except his only possession, the cat. So the cat was sent aboard as the 'item' to be sold on Mr Whittington's behalf.

Now, there emerged a new villain in the form of Mr Fitzwarren's cook, who made Dick's life miserable. He was cruel and evil, and got sadistic pleasure in punishing Dick. Unable to take his torture any longer, Dick decided to run away from London. Nursing the wounds of his broken dreams and hopes, as he turned to leave the city, feeling defeated and miserable, the famous Bow Bells of London rang out. It was as if they were recapturing the magic of Dick's forgotten London dreams. They seemed to call out to him, 'Come back, Dick Whittington, thrice to-be lord mayor of London!'

Regaining a foothold on the magic of his dream, Dick wiped away his tears, and with newfound determination retraced his steps back to the city. He braved the insults and the misery, overcame newer hurdles and falls, and looked ahead.

When Mr Fitzwarren's ship returned from its maiden voyage, the captain reported that Dick's cat had been sold for a small fortune to an eastern king whose palace had been infested with rats. Dick took the money and requested his master to teach him the fine art of being a successful trader. Mightily pleased by the young lad's trust in him, Mr Fitzwarren took the boy under his wings and taught him all the tricks of the trade to make him a successful businessman. He also gave his daughter Alice in marriage to this smart young man who had sought refuge with him as an orphan.

The prophecy of the Bow Bells, it appeared was coming true. Starting as a flourishing trader, Dick soon rose to become a councillor, and eventually, was elected lord mayor of the City of London. He went on to occupy this august office for a record three times, becoming an aspirational icon for all determined young men whose dream was to make it big!

As we saw, Dick's character as a folk tale figure was based on the life of Sir Richard Whittington, a philanthropist, trader and mayor of London. Sir Richard Whittington was four times lord mayor of London, and also became a member of parliament and a sheriff of London. He too, like Dick, married an heiress, but being childless, he bequeathed his enormous fortune to form the Charity of Sir Richard Whittington, which continues to assist people in need.

The Whittington Hospital at Archway in the London Borough of Islington and a small statue of a cat along Highgate Hill further commemorate this legendary figure.

Understanding

Have you ever tried the much acclaimed technique of active visualisation? It is one of the surest ways to success and involves 'reprogramming' the mind to think positively. Psychologists tell us that the mind 'thinks' largely in the form of images. When we fill the mind with positive visuals, positive energy is generated to help us succeed in whatever we are focusing on.

Have you ever had to wait for your lunch or dinner on a festival day while the food is being prepared at home for a special pooja? You conjure up images of all the hot, delicious, nutritious food that is going to be put on the table, which you and your family members will share with great appetite. You can almost smell its tempting aroma. When you visualise the delicacies, the sweets, the savouries and the mouth-watering dishes on offer, does that not make you hungry?

Images are indeed very powerful! But you can also use them to improve your health, heal wounds, pass exams, stand first in class, attain your goals and achieve anything that you put your mind onto.

Burn victims have been taught to visualise their skin as clean, clear and baby-soft. They train their mind to see the burnt patch growing smaller and smaller, until it vanishes into thin air.

Fracture patients see their bones healing and joining together. They see themselves walking, running or using their broken limbs normally.

Even cancer victims are taught to practise this technique that combines the effect of strong visualisation with powerful thought energy.

Warming Up

Today, decide to be a witness. Just detach yourself from your mind and watch how far your thoughts can take you—upward or downward! When you become aware of your thoughts, you see the impact they have on your emotions. They will also have an impact on your breathing, your heart rate and your overall mood. It is only when you become aware of their power, can you learn to control them!

Words of Wisdom

We are formed and moulded by our thoughts. Those whose minds are shaped by selfless thoughts, give joy when they speak or act. Joy follows them like a shadow that never leaves them.

—*Gautama Buddha*

We are what our thoughts have made us, so take care about what you think. Words are secondary. Thoughts live; they travel far.

—*Swami Vivekananda*

Lesson 5

NOT STUMBLING BLOCKS, BUT STEPPING STONES

Problems and challenges are not dead ends; they are only bends in the road. Problems are not stumbling blocks, rather they can be the stepping stones to a better, richer and more radiant life. Often, problems become the door through which God enters our lives. We encase ourselves in hard shells, which keeps God away. But problems can crack these shells and make way for divinity to bless our lives.

To most Indians, the great epic, *Mahabharata*, represents the archetypal struggle between good and evil. As we know, the Pandava brothers stand for the good, while their sworn enemies, the Kauravas, symbolise all that is evil—envy, jealousy, greed, falsehood, treachery and injustice.

If we look at the *Mahabharata* from this perspective, we can clearly see the trials, tribulations and ordeals that the Pandavas were put through from the beginning till the end. Let me sum up these trials to refresh your memory of this much admired story:

The Pandavas' ordeals began very early on. Their uncle, Dhritarashtra was a weak and biased ruler. He was disturbed by the growing popularity of the Pandavas as this put his sons in a bad light. His wife Gandhari's brother, Shakuni, plotted and conspired with his nephews to do away with their cousins. A palace of wax was constructed at Shakuni's behest, and the Pandavas were invited to stay there along with their mother, Kunti. Suspecting foul play, the Pandavas, however, had dug a secret tunnel to serve as an exit from the wax palace. And it was through this tunnel that they escaped to safety, when the palace was set on fire by the deceiving Kauravas.

Realising that their lives continued to be in danger as the Kauravas were ruthless, Kunti and her sons disguised themselves as mendicant Brahmins and travelled from place to place. Wandering thus, they reached the kingdom of Drupad, where the beautiful princess Draupadi was to marry the most skilful archer who would emerge as a winner in a contest of valour. As we know, it was Arjuna who won this conquest, but at Kunti's behest, Draupadi was married off to all the five princes.

Dhritarashtra was then constrained to invite the Pandavas back to Hastinapur, and also make Yudhisthira the ruler of an adjoining land. Here, under the guidance of Lord Krishna, the Pandavas ruled wisely and well. They built a beautiful city called Indraprastha, with a magnificent palace, where Yudhisthira performed the Rajasuya Yajna. Many kings and princes attended the event and lavished praise on the Pandavas.

Duryodhana was so envious of his cousins' good fortune, that right after returning to Hastinapur, he plotted and connived with his uncle, Shakuni and brother Dushasan, to strip the Pandavas of their kingdom, power and wealth, and to drive them away from their hearth and home. In line with their evil designs, the Kauravas conceived to trick them through a deadly game of dice. Accordingly, they issued an invitation to the Pandavas to play a game of dice—a royal custom which no prince could refuse. Shakuni then used loaded dice, rolling it every time in his own favour, and the Pandavas lost heavily at every throw. It was unfortunate that Yudhisthira could not check himself and stop playing; the dice game was his weakness. As the game progressed, the Pandavas lost everything they had, including their kingdom, their crown and even their freedom. In a last desperate gamble, prompted by the evil Shakuni, Yudhisthira offered Draupadi as the wager, and she too fell victim to the false dice. The Pandavas and their wife, all then became the slaves of the Kauravas.

In a fit of vengeful malice, Duryodhana ordered Dushasan to drag Draupadi by her hair to the court. While she protested vehemently, he told Dushasan to strip her of her clothes. The elders of the Kuru dynasty, Bhishma, Dhritarashtra and their Guru, Dronacharya sat in silence, as mute spectators while the lady's modesty was being outraged. Draupadi's five husbands simply hung their heads in shame and grief. Only Vidura, the blind king's cousin, dared to protest, but to no avail. Draupadi then prayed to Lord Krishna, who came to her aid instantly, and saved her dignity from being outraged.

A little too late, King Dhritarashtra woke up to the horror of the events taking place in his court. He used his sovereign power to set the Pandavas and Draupadi free, but one condition remained. As losers in the game, they would be forced to spend twelve years in the forest, and the thirteenth year incognito, before they could reclaim their lost kingdom. If they were detected, the whole cycle of exile would have to be repeated.

The Pandavas spent twelve long years deep in the forest. Their one source of joy and support was the constant, never failing guidance and friendship of Lord Krishna. During their exile, the Pandavas had many daring adventures and dealt with myriad problems. Yet they made numerous friends and gained many well-wishers. When the thirteenth year began, they decided to seek refuge at the court of King Virata, all of them, suitably disguised to prevent detection.

Yudhisthira became a dice-player to entertain the king. Arjuna donned female garb and was appointed the dance and music teacher of Princess Uttara. Bhima worked as the royal cook. Nakula and Sahadeva took charge of the stables. Draupadi was appointed the queen's maid-in-waiting, calling herself Sairandhari.

We know the familiar story well, and we are aware that the final victory belonged to the Pandavas. But what obstacles they had to surmount, how many problems they faced before that victory could be accomplished! And, what a heavy price they had paid for that final victory, killing their own brother Karna, failing to prevent the treacherous killing of the valiant Abhimanyu, seeing their entire family being destroyed, losing each and every one of their children!

They may have been the children of devas; they were royal princes and great warriors, emerging as brave heroes, yet they went through their share of human suffering. The Pandavas did not break down, but evolved through their suffering; they drew closer and closer to Sri Krishna, and by the end of the story, as we know, they relinquished all worldly possessions and powers to seek their own liberation.

Understanding

Are you facing a major problem or challenge? Do you want to change the circumstances surrounding you so that they suit you? Do you get frustrated and desperate when things don't go your way?

Don't try to change things that are not in your control. Instead, try altering your perspective in life. Look afresh at your problems, elevate your thinking, try a different approach, work on your attitude, re-examine your course of action. Perhaps, a new way can help.

Today, try focusing on a solution, instead of the problem.

Warming Up

Choose an incident from the life of a saint, a martyr or a great personality. Jesus Christ, Gautama Buddha, Hussain, the martyr of Karbala, Guru Tegh Bahadur, Sri Ramakrishna Parmahansa, Mahatma Gandhi are some of the names that spring readily to mind. None of these great souls had an easy time; their paths were not strewn with flowers. They faced the kind of problems and challenges that might have left us crushed and defeated. Ponder on the magnanimity of their spirits; marvel at the strength of their souls, which enabled them to surmount all those extraordinary challenges and forge their way forward, 'Godward'.

Words of Wisdom

Stand up, be bold, be strong. Take the whole responsibility on your own shoulders, and know that you are the creator of your own destiny. All the strength and succour you want is within yourself. Therefore, make your own future.

—*Swami Vivekananda*

Life's ups and downs provide windows of opportunity to determine your values and goals. Think of using all obstacles as stepping stones to build the life you want.

—*Marsha Sinetar*

Difficulties are opportunities to better things, they are stepping stones to greater experience. Perhaps some day you will be thankful for some temporary failure in a particular direction. When one door closes, another always opens; as a natural law it has to be, to balance.

—*Brian Adams*

Lesson 6

LOVE ONE ANOTHER!

Neither rites nor rituals, neither creeds nor ceremonies are needed to improve the condition of the world. All that is needed is—that we love one another.

In the Hoshiarpur district of Punjab lived a holy man, a sanyasi, whose simple life and profound teachings attracted many seekers, who came to live with him as disciples and were called *brahmacharis*. Many more followers flocked to attend the sanyasi's daily satsang. They sought his guidance in tackling their spiritual issues, and often brought their families along to meet the holy seer and seek his blessings. Some of them got together and built an ashram for their guru and his disciples. Soon this ashram became the centre of pilgrimage for thousands of followers who looked up to the sanyasi as their spiritual master. The ashram grew rapidly, and soon turned into a very busy place. Local businessmen contributed generously to feed hundreds of poor people who thronged to the ashram daily. Food and accommodation was provided to disciples who came to visit their master; annual congregations and spiritual retreats were held regularly. Over a period, the ashram evolved into a tiny self-contained township that attracted thousands of visitors.

As time passed, the sanyasi attained the Lotus Feet of the Lord. His appointed successor, a quiet and gentle monk then took charge. The new head monk was determined to follow his master's teachings in letter and spirit, and uphold all the traditions of the ashram. But this did not happen. For there was something missing in the ashram now. Petty politics and quarrels began to take root in the ashram; the younger monks and the *bramhachari* disciples could not see eye to eye; arguments marred the proceedings of important meetings. The administration of the ashram began to suffer: The treasurer blamed the manager and the manager blamed the secretary; even the 'feed-the-poor' programme ran into trouble. The influx to the ashram gradually began to dwindle. The ashram programmes turned lacklustre; even the attendance at the daily satsang thinned. Blind to all this, the chief disciples continued to quarrel, relentlessly blaming each other for the sorry state of affairs at the ashram. The overcrowded ashram then became a deserted place. Only fifteen to twenty people now remained—the head monk, the chief disciples and few senior office bearers who were in charge of the day-to-day running of the ashram.

The chief monk was deeply saddened. He searched and searched for a way to salvage the precious spiritual inheritance of his beloved master, the sanyasi. Ultimately, he decided to seek the counsel of a holy sage who lived in Rishikesh. This sage had visited the ashram in its flourishing days, and bonded very well with the sanyasi.

So the monk reached the *kutiya* of the friendly sage in Rishikesh, where he was warmly welcomed by the holy man. Here, in a private meeting with the sage, the distraught monk poured out his heart. He begged the seer to suggest a way to stop the ashram from disintegrating further.

The sage heard him out quietly, taking in all the details of the sordid affair at the ashram. He then advised the monk to retire for the night after spending some time in quiet prayer. 'I shall do likewise,' he said, 'and we shall see, the new day will bring with it God's guidance to tackle the problem. Come to me soon after the morning prayer, and I shall tell you what I think.'

The chief monk followed the sage's advice. He spent an hour or so in silent prayer, pleading to God and his guru to intervene. They must ensure he never had the misfortune to preside over the closure of his beloved guru's ashram.

Next morning, he was ready and waiting outside the sage's *kutiya*, and was summoned soon enough. The sage looked him squarely in the eye, and said, 'You must go back to the ashram and take every step you can think of to revive it to its former glory. For I must reveal to you, it is not the place you take it to be. The Lord has chosen your ashram to appear in one of his secret incarnations. Even right now, Lord Vishnu is with you in your ashram. He is one amongst you, though you may not be able to perceive Him with your clouded vision. But when the veil lifts from your eyes, you will surely see Him. I entreat you, do what you must, but do not drive away the Lord from your midst with petty quarrels and internal politics. Unite to rebuild your ashram, make it a worthy abode of the Lord who has chosen to come amongst you. Return to the ashram at once, and set an example for your disciples. Remember, God is with you; He is watching you; He is watching over you.'

The chief monk turned speechless with amazement. Lord Vishnu was amongst them in the ashram! Who could he be? One of the monks? One among the *brahmacharis?* One of the staff? Try as he might, he simply could not 'place' the chosen man. Each and every inmate of the ashram appeared to him deeply flawed, and quite unfit to be the secret incarnation of the Lord. But then the Lord was the King of a thousand *leelas*: It was a small matter for Him to disguise His omnipotence and omniscience, and appear to the world as an ordinary human being with all the common weaknesses of such a man. He could be a monk, He could be a disciple, He could even be the cook or the watchman or the manager!

When the chief monk returned to the ashram, he was a changed man. He was no longer the withdrawn, aloof monk who was content to let things drift from bad to worse. He was a man with a mission; he had to ensure that the Lord who had come to live in his ashram, should not leave the place in disgust!

When they sat down in the satsang hall for their evening prayer, the chief monk cast his eyes around furtively, trying to spot the Lord. All heads were bowed down in prayer; anyone of them could be the Lord, he thought to himself. Each and every member looked *satvik*, devout and sincere. 'I will not let my guru's congregation disperse,' he vowed to himself. 'It must be my guru who has pleaded with the Lord to come down amongst us so that we may change our ways and become worthy of His Grace.'

There was such a pronounced change in the chief monk's demeanour and attitude that it had a very powerful effect on the rest of the inmates. Suddenly, the vibrations changed, the atmosphere grew more peaceful and positive. It was not long before the chief monk shared his 'intelligence' with the senior monks and disciples. Everyone was spellbound. They began to look at each other with new respect and love. If the Lord was indeed amongst them, they were determined that they would give Him no cause to reject their devotion. And since it was impossible to fathom His *leelas* and decipher His real identity, they felt the only thing they could do under the circumstances was to treat everyone with the greatest love and respect. Why, He had come upon this earth as a fish, a tortoise, a boar and a man-lion, he could be the cook, the chowkidar, the manager or indeed one of the *brahmacharis*! There was only one thing to do now, pour out all their love, affection and respect for each and every inmate so that the Lord was sure to receive His due!

Need I say that the ashram became, once again, a centre of radiance, devotion, love and *atma shakti*!

Understanding

Here is a wonderful attitude tip to help you retain that smile permanently on your face. Often, in our daily lives, we come across people who speak, act or behave in ways that are hurtful to us. Maybe, you have a colleague who is constantly trying to put you down, or a cranky neighbour who never smiles at you. Perhaps, your brother or sister keeps picking fights with you, or you have a spouse who is ever ready to find fault with everything you do. The thing to remember at all times, though, is that most people don't really mean to be nasty. But they may be going through a rough time themselves, and this may be what prevents them from being kind and courteous to others. Many people are troubled deep inside their hearts by problems they cannot solve, challenges they cannot face. They are troubled and they do not want to show it. Try not to take their words and actions at face value. Don't take it personally. Next time, someone acts unreasonably, say this to yourself, 'There is a good reason why he or she is behaving this way. I don't know that reason, but if I did, perhaps, I would understand him better.' This will help you to be kinder and less judgmental.

Warming Up

It is only when we are recipients of love that we can become dispensers of love. First you must become aware of God's abundant love for you, simply by realising how God has blessed you in very many ways. Once you realise how much He loves you, it will be an easy step to become a channel of that pure love.

Further, when we come to realise how unconditional God's love for us is despite our worthlessness, we learn to be more tolerant, loving and forgiving.

His love for you is absolute and unconditional. Spread it in the same unconditional way to every person who crosses your path today.

WORDS OF WISDOM

We have not come into the world to be
numbered; we have been created for a purpose;
for great things—to love and be loved.

It is not the magnitude of our actions,
but the amount of love that is put into them
that matters.

Spread love everywhere you go. Let no one ever
come to you without leaving happier.

We cannot always do great things, but we can do
small things with great love.

—*Mother Teresa*

Lesson 7

WHERE IS GOD?

Are you anxious to find God? Then you must be prepared to lose yourself! Do you want God to be yours? Then you must first become His!

There's a moving story surrounding Sri Chaitanya Mahaprabhu, about the time he stayed in Puri. Vasudeva was a humble, pious and good-natured Brahmin, but was afflicted by the loathed curse of leprosy. This disease forced him to stay as far away from people as he could for it had completely disfigured him, and a foul smell emanated from his putrid sores.

Vasudeva was a true Vaishnava for whom ahimsa was a way of life. He could not bear to see maggots crawling on his sores, and dropping off when they could no longer feed. He would thus carefully pick them up and deposit them in a safe corner where people would not trample upon them!

One day, he heard that Sri Chaitanya Mahaprabhu was to visit the Kurma Temple in the vicinity. He longed to have a darshan of the saint from afar. But the milling crowds in the temple drove him away, saying that Sri Chaitanya had left much earlier. Depressed and dejected, he fell down, exclaiming, 'O Krishna, have You no hope to offer me?'

This fervent plea of a Krishna devotee reached Sri Chaitanya's ears; he rushed back to the temple, and seeing Vasudeva, lifted the afflicted bhakta in his arms, embracing him with deep affection and compassion. Neither the Lord nor His saints care about the wealth or the physical appearance of a true devotee. The multi-millionaire and the poor beggar are not materially different in the Lord's eyes, even if the world may choose to think otherwise. To Sri Chaitanya, it did not matter that he was embracing a leper, an outcast who was shunned and reviled by the crowds. All he saw in the leper was a fellow Krishna bhakta. And a miracle came to pass! Vasudeva's leprosy vanished, leaving no scars. He turned hale and hearty with skin that was unblemished and a body restored to vitality and good health!

Moved to tears, Vasudeva then begged Chaitanya Mahaprabhu to let him remain a leper, lest he should grow proud of himself and forget the valuable lessons of humility and compassion he had learnt as a social outcast. 'When I had no one to lean on, no one to call my own, the Lord became my friend, companion and my constant support. I had Him, and Him alone to call my own. Now that I am restored to good health and vitality, I shall have many friends and companions surrounding me. But, I would rather be a leper and have the Lord as my one support than be of this world and lose His Grace,' he requested with folded hands.

However, Sri Chaitanya assured him, 'My child! You have the Grace of Lord Krishna. You have known suffering and rejection, and yet you clung to His Lotus Feet with love and devotion. You will never be one of those people puffed up with vanity and pride, as long as you recite the name of the Lord with love and devotion. Therefore, let the Lord's name be on your lips constantly. Lord Krishna has blessed you with humility and compassion for all living creatures, even towards those maggots who fed on your body. Repeat His Name Divine, and chant His name to everyone you meet, so that they too may be blessed by His Grace!'

Understanding

Many of us make a journal of our day-to-day activities and thoughts in our personal diaries. Businessmen and executives often maintain official diaries or appointment logs where details of important meetings and deadlines are carefully recorded. Even schools and colleges have academic calendars where planned events and programmes are noted. But have you ever thought of maintaining a personal journal for your communications with the Lord?

Keeping such a journal can enhance your devotion. As we know, a journal entry can take many forms, it can be a mundane account of all that happened to you, perhaps, a record of all feelings and thoughts that beset you, or it could simply be an expression of your highest and noblest thoughts, your introspections on life and living! The journal I refer to, can be your personal communication with God. In this journal, you can pen down your inspirations, those personal messages sent by God when you are sitting in prayer, or even as you move about in your daily chores. It lets you share your innermost feelings with God, and hand over your troubles and worries to Him in a tangible manner that's official and on-the-record. It becomes, in essence, a record of your spiritual journey with God.

Warming Up

Today, in the course of your daily work routine, find at least two occasions when you hand your life over to the Lord. Great saints and sages have done this their entire lives; we can at least begin with small occasions. All you need to do is subdue your will, and stop resisting the opinions and wishes of others. Instead of asserting yourself aggressively, embrace the spirit of acceptance of God's Will. To begin with, pick up just two occasions. It will not be easy! But it is worth a try. Discover the joy of losing yourself in God!

Words of Wisdom

But they for whom I am the supreme goal, who do all work renouncing self for Me and meditate on Me with single-hearted devotion, these I will swiftly rescue from death's vast sea, for their consciousness has entered into Me.

—*Srimad Bhagavad Gita*

Give me the boon of devotion, O my Guru, O God of Gods; nothing more do I desire save Thy service day and night.

—*Kabir*

Lesson 8

Closer, My God, to Thee!

How may we know that we are drawing closer to God?

The closer we draw to God, the more tender and compassionate become our hearts to the needs of those around us.

This story took place in those early halcyon days of Christianity, when the faith was spreading far and wide in the Roman Empire, which extended right upto West Asia. Mariam was an old lady who lived all alone in one of the small hamlets near Jerusalem. No one knew how old she was; neither could she enlighten them on that point. She was lean, emaciated and almost bent double with aches resulting from bone diseases that malnourished women are prone to in their old age. She eked out a living babysitting infants in the hamlet when their mothers were busy with housework; for their part, they offered her the remains of their daily food, and Mariam survived on the leftovers. She hardly ever left home; the babies were brought to her and left in her care, and when the mothers returned to collect their babies, they brought along some bread or broth or greens that they could spare for the old woman. And thus, life went on for Mariam, who said she was only counting days till she would be finally called to appear before the Lord.

One evening, the village trader who had gone to Jerusalem on work, returned with some news for the village. A famous saint was visiting Jerusalem. He would be holding a public mass that all the faithful in the Christian community were called upon to attend. The saint would be in Jerusalem only for a day or two, then move onwards in his journey across the holy land, right up to Constantinople.

Mariam was thrilled to hear this. She decided to go to Jerusalem and attend the public mass where she could catch a glimpse of this saint. It was just what she needed to prepare herself to face death, which she was convinced, was not far off now. I must go to Jerusalem and receive the saint's blessings before I die, she thought. Even if I die on the way, God will bless me and take my soul to Heaven. It was truly a God-given opportunity, attend mass, take the sacrament and prepare to face her Creator! The Lord, in His goodness and kindness was making this possible for her!

When she announced her decision to her neighbours, they grew concerned for her. 'Grandmother!' they cried in unison, 'You don't know what you are talking about! Jerusalem is a good four-hour walk from our village! How can you get there in your weak condition? Stay put here in the safety of your home and worship the God who dwells in your heart. He does not want you to go out to Jerusalem to pray to Him. Who is to say what will happen to you on the way? Who will take care of you if you should fall sick?'

But Mariam was determined to seek her salvation by setting out for Jerusalem. 'God will take me there, and He will care for me on the way, if anything befalls me.'

'Will God send His Son down again on this earth to care for an old woman?' mocked one of the young women.

'The Son of God does not need to trouble Himself so for a poor old woman like me,' replied Mariam in high spirits. 'Some of His kind-hearted children, my fellow human beings will do it for Him.'

And so, on the appointed day, Mariam actually set out for Jerusalem, bent double, holding strongly onto her stick for support. The first fifteen minutes were actually very easy. Her energy and enthusiasm seemed to propel her forward on its own steam. But after some time, the aches and pains caught up with her again. Her joints began to hurt and her legs crumbled, unable to carry her lean frame. An hour later, her eyes lost focus; she felt the world spinning around her and sank to the ground, gasping in pain and exhaustion. There she lay, beneath a tree by the wayside, writhing in pain.

'Help, O please help me!' she called out to those who were passing by.

The road to Jerusalem was filled with travellers that day, all going to the holy city to attend the public mass. Rich people came in their wagons; wealthy farmers and traders were on their mules; hundreds of men, women and children had decided to turn this holy day into a holiday for the whole family. Young men talked and laughed loudly as they walked along. But no one bothered to pay any attention to the old and helpless woman.

A wealthy merchant happened to come by then. He ordered his man to pull up his cart, and peering out at Mariam, asked in concern, 'Mother, what can I do for you? Why are you lying here all alone by the wayside? Where are the members of your family? How could they abandon you in this condition?'

'I have no family to speak of,' said Mariam with tear-filled eyes. 'I am only counting my last days, and all I want is to go to the holy city of Jerusalem and have a glimpse of the saint and attend my final mass before God sends for me, which I know will be very soon now.'

The merchant was overcome with pity for the old woman. 'Let us take the old lady along with us in the wagon,' he suggested to his wife. 'The Lord asks us to love our neighbours as we love ourselves.'

'Stop being so stupid,' hissed his wife, who was seated next to him in the wagon. 'How can we take this old decrepit female with us? What will people say when she gets down with us? Why, they might even think that she is my mother, and that I come from peasant stock! Just curb your generous instincts and tell the wagoner to drive on!'

Mariam did not overhear this conversation, but she saw the wagon drive away and understood what must have happened. Her anxious eyes searched for another soul who may be willing to help her. And then, all of a sudden, much singing, cheering and loud laughter rang in her ears. Around the bend in the road, marched up a group of young and happy lads, bursting with holiday cheer and spirit. Her hopes rising, she called out to the merry bunch, 'My dear children! Please let me walk with you. Lend me the support of your strong arms so that I may reach Jerusalem in your gay company and greet the saint who comes to us with God's message.'

'Where shall we walk with you?' one of them asked her, smirking. 'Shall we walk you to your grave? Because that's where you seem to be headed. As for Jerusalem, shouldn't you be a little practical and think how far your legs can carry you?' The whole waiting bunch of young men laughed out loud, and passed her by.

A robust farmer and his wife came along, next, but they had two children holding on to their hands, and excused themselves saying they were not free to support her. It was noon by now, and the sun shone directly overhead, making Mariam weak with heat and exhaustion. She grew faint with thirst and hunger.

'Mother, mother, are you alright?' a kind voice whispered in her ear then. 'Here, let me help you sit up. Would you like a sip of water? Here is the cool and clear water I filled from a spring, just a while ago.' And a pitcher was held up to her lips, from which she drank gratefully.

She looked up and saw a young priest, dressed in sackcloth, as monks used to wear in those days. He told her that he too was on his way to Jerusalem to greet the saint. Propping her up against the tree trunk, he shared his bread with her, and then helped her stand up and prepare for the journey ahead. When he realised she could not walk two steps without groaning, he offered caringly, 'Mother, you must let me carry you on my back, for I see that you are too frail to walk. But, like you, I too feel very strongly that you should be blessed by the grace of the saint who has come all the way only to help people like you. So let me carry you along, and we will reach Jerusalem in time for the mass.'

Thus it was that Mariam—God bless her soul—was able to reach Jerusalem that evening. The duo was stunned to see the vast ocean of people who had travelled to the holy city for a glimpse of the saint. There seemed to be hundreds and thousands of people out there in the vast open air ground, all waiting to participate in the mass. Even as they watched, a roar of greeting went up from the collected throng. The saint of God had just risen to address the people. The priest was a tall man, and could see the saint, but realising that the bent old woman on his back could not catch what was happening, he offered kindly, 'Mother, I am going to put you on my shoulders, then you too can see what is happening.'

Mariam stood on the priest's strong shoulders, and through cascading tears of joy and piety, watched the saint raise his hands to bless the crowd. To her joy and amazement, the saint resembled the kind priest who had helped her reach the holy city. 'May God bless you, may God bless you,' she sobbed as she realised that the kindness and compassion of the priest revealed that he too, was a saint in the making!

The merchant and his wife were standing on the seats of their wagon; the rowdy youths she had approached for help earlier that day, formed a human pyramid to catch a glimpse of the saint. To their utter shame and amazement, they saw the bent figure of the old woman, with her wrinkled face and grey hair, in place of the saint. Their conscience pricked them then, and they hung their heads in shame.

As for the priest, he silently thanked the Lord for this opportunity to be instrumental in the healing of an old woman. He then strained to see the face of the saint. To his amazement, he saw instead the figure of Christ, holding out his hands and saying, 'Come unto me, all ye that are weary and heavy laden, and I will refresh you.' He was, indeed, the most blessed of all the pilgrims to Jerusalem that year—because he loved all the Lord's children as much as he loved the Lord Himself. He had done to the least of God's people, what he would have done unto God Himself!

UNDERSTANDING

Have you heard of DHEA and cortisol? These are hormones produced in the brain, and their ratio determines the 'mood' or 'attitude' of people. Quite simply, when DHEA levels are high, and cortisol levels are low, people are relaxed and happy; when the ratio of cortisol increases, depression and stress result.

Researchers have found that people who actively practise compassion and go out of their way to help others, produce 100 per cent more DHEA, which is also a hormone that counteracts the aging process, and 23 per cent less cortisol—the stress hormone.

How can we develop the spirit of compassion? One easy way to do this is to simply 'put ourselves in others' shoes', as the saying goes. Think of what you have in common with others, rather than how they are different from you, and how you cannot get along with them, focus on the similarities and ignore the differences.

Experts recommend an easy five-step exercise to try when you meet friends and strangers. Practise this discreetly, and see the difference for yourself:

Step 1: 'This person too, like me, is seeking happiness in his life.'

Step 2: 'Just like me, this person is also trying to avoid suffering in his life.'

Step 3: 'Like me, this person has also known sadness, loneliness and despair.'

Step 4: 'Just like me, this person is seeking to fulfil his needs.'

Step 5: 'Just like me, this person is learning about life.'

Warming Up

Make today the day of compassion—find ways to express your love and compassion to every human being, creature and object. If you see a bird, send her your love; if you meet a friend, express your love and appreciation and tell him what he has meant in your life; hug your parents or spouse and tell them how much you love and appreciate all that they are doing for you. If you use a computer or a car, treat it gently and lovingly. If you see someone lost in thought, bless him, smile at him and send a silent prayer for his welfare.

Words of Wisdom

When we feel love and kindness towards others,
it not only makes others feel loved and cared for,
but it also helps us to develop inner happiness
and peace.

—The Dalai Lama

The more we come out and do good to others,
the more our hearts will be purified, and God
will be in them.

—Swami Vivekananda

Have you had a kindness shown? Pass it on;
'Twas not given for thee alone, Pass it on;
Let it travel down the years,
Let it wipe another's tears.
Pass it on.

—Rev Henry Burton

Lesson 9

Cure for the Heart

What is the best exercise for the heart? Reach down and lift up as many as you can.

Mrs Warren-Smith was a very wealthy socialite, who, like many of her rich friends, 'was under therapy'. Every alternate day, she would wear her most expensive and fashionable suit and visit the plush offices of her psychiatrist, lie on his couch and vent her grievances, listing all the unkind cuts that life had dealt her. 'Nobody loves me, nobody understands me,' was her constant refrain. Sometimes, she would complain, 'I have lost my appetite; I just don't want to eat any more.' At other times, it was, 'I just can't get to sleep! I am afflicted with severe insomnia.'

Her psychiatrist, Dr Cooper allowed her to have her way for the first six weeks of therapy, and heard out her whole litany of complaints. On her following visit, he informed that her actual treatment would begin from that point. Her next session, he said would be with a 'happiness expert'. Mrs Warren-Smith was very pleased. She was getting fed up with the good doctor's unresponsive demeanour and silent note-taking. Maybe, the happiness expert would be more sympathetic. At any rate, it would be nice to recite all her old complaints to a new person.

The doctor opened the door of the consulting room and called out, 'Mrs Jones, would you please come in now?' She was shocked to see the lady who entered with her broom and mop and bucket. Why, she had seen this woman before; it was none other than the cleaning lady who was wiping or sweeping or dusting in the lobby of the posh building where Dr Cooper and other doctors had their clinics. Mrs Jones put away her cleaning materials and took her seat near the couch, as the doctor had indicated. She folded her hands and put them primly on her knees. Mrs Warren-Smith noticed that her hands were rough and calloused, her nails were not polished or painted, she wore absolutely no make-up and her dress was plain and simple. But her eyes sparkled, and the most lovely smile played upon her lips.

'Tell us Mrs Jones,' the doctor began, 'are you happy?'

'Yes, thank you doctor,' smiled the lady. 'I am very happy indeed.'

'And how is your appetite these days?' the doctor continued. 'Do you eat well?'

'The good Lord blesses me with two square meals a day,' beamed Mrs Jones, 'and I am happy to say, I do justice to what He sends me.'

'And, do you sleep well at night?'

'The moment my head hits the pillow, I nod off, and I only wake up when the sunlight creeps into my room.'

'Tell me Mrs Jones, were you always this happy?'

'My dear sir, you know how miserable I was when I lost my husband and son in that railroad accident five years ago,' said Mrs Jones, wiping away a tear. 'You must remember, I even stopped coming to work.'

'Please go on,' urged the doctor, 'tell us what happened after that?'

'Well, I sank into a mire of depression and misery,' said Mrs Jones. 'I could not eat, I could not sleep and I hated meeting people or even talking to anyone. I shut myself up in my little flat, and became a recluse.

'One evening, I heard a pathetic mewing and scratching noise at the door. It was a little kitten, who had been separated from its mother and then abandoned by the family. The little creature was so lost and so scared that my heart melted at her plight. I took her inside and gave her some milk in a saucer. She lapped it all up in a jiffy and gave me a look that made me hug her. I decided to take her in and make her my pet and my companion. You won't believe how she was transformed in a day's time with all the love and care I gave her! And, as for me, I found a new purpose for my existence! Far from being an abandoned, sad woman, I found that I was in a position to help other creatures, who were worse off than me.

'Soon, the thought came to my mind that if a little animal could be so happy with my kindness, how much more happiness I could offer to my fellow human beings. So, the next day, I baked some cookies and took them over to the old lady who lived upstairs. How delighted she was, and how delighted I was to see her so pleased!

'And that was how my new life began. I did whatever I could to please people. I baked cakes and biscuits for old and young neighbours; I began to babysit for my younger friends. I volunteered to care for the animals at the stray dogs shelter. I returned to work because I needed more money to make more people happy. And since then, sir, I have not looked back!'

'But my good woman,' Mrs Warren-Smith intervened to protest, 'you are not an expert. You cannot take on the cares and anxieties of people with complex problems!'

'True, madam, I am not an expert at treating people,' confessed Mrs Jones. 'But I can smile! And I can offer a shoulder for people to cry on. And that doesn't need expertise now, does it madam?'

Mrs Warren-Smith stared speechlessly at the cheerful, bright-eyed cleaning woman. She had indeed discovered the secret to happiness! She simply had to make others happy, and the happiness that went out from her to others, would come back to her manifold.

Understanding

Seek out opportunities today, to help others. Do not frown at your fellow motorists or the traffic cop; instead, smile at them cheerfully. Smile at people you encounter on the stairs and in the lobby. Share a joke with your colleagues. Exchange pleasantries with the staff in your office. Offer random acts of kindness to someone—move a chair or offer the first place in the queue, carry a heavy bag perhaps, for someone.

When you make an effort to help others, you are spreading positive energy. The people you help are sure to be touched by this energy. They may even decide to spread this further by repeating your acts of kindness to others they meet. You will set off a powerful wave of kindness and positive energy!

Warming Up

Look out for opportunities today to be of service to others. If you find opportunities, consider yourself fortunate. Even though you may only do a little thing, like serving a glass of water or waiting. perhaps for an old man wanting to cross the road during peak time traffic, make that effort to do it wholeheartedly, and you will be richly rewarded.

Words of Wisdom

Remember that when you leave this earth you can take nothing of what you have received, but only what you have given: A full heart, enriched by honest service, love, sacrifice and courage.

—*Saint Francis of Assisi*

Help as many as you can but if you cannot help, at least do not hurt anyone.

—*The Dalai Lama*

Never look down on anybody unless you're helping him up.

—*Jesse Jackson*

Lesson 10

Convert Misfortunes into Blessings

Misfortunes are blessings if we handle them well. They are like knives which hurt or help as we hold them by the blade or handle.

Long ago, there was an ascetic who lived in a small village in northern India. He lived on the alms the villagers thoughtfully provided. His needs were simple. He spent the daytime mostly in prayer and silent meditation. In the evening, he would freely share his thoughts with the villagers who came to him, as to a satsang. Every time people approached him with their problems and grievances, the ascetic dispensed advice and practical solutions. It would be no exaggeration to say that the entire village looked upon him as a guru and guardian of their welfare.

Sometimes, mothers would haul their naughty or disobedient children up to him, and he would narrate to them stories that inspired the young ones to behave well. Feuding brothers would present before him their dispute over some ancestral property, and the seer would offer wise counsel to settle their quarrel amicably. When people expected him to cure mysterious illnesses, the old man would smear holy ash on the forehead of the sick, and offer miracle water that he had blessed by reciting the *naam jaap*. Rarely did these remedies fail the villagers. In time, they learned to respect his wisdom and sagely advice.

One evening, the villagers walked up to the ascetic with very worried faces. They reported something quite strange. Overnight, every rooster, hen and chicken in the village had succumbed to some mysterious illness. 'Swamiji, we are shocked and very upset with this loss,' they cried. 'All our poultry is gone, and with it, a sizable source of our livelihood. Why did all this happen? And what shall we do?'

The ascetic closed his eyes and pondered for a minute or two. Then he pronounced, 'Whatever has happened, has happened because it is the Lord's Will. Accept it, for it must be for your own good.'

The villagers had much faith in his words and dispersed quietly, accepting it as the seer said.

A few days later, another disaster struck the village. All the dogs in the village fell to a strange and mysterious illness. Again, the distraught villagers rushed to their guru and narrated the strange and untoward happenings. 'What is happening to us, Swamiji?' they asked in unison. 'Is it a portend of something terrible that is to befall us?'

Once again, the saint spent a few moments in silent prayer. Then he said to the villagers, 'Go in peace; all that happens, happens with His Will. And His Will is the best for us all.'

The villagers were now a little perplexed. Their guru had always given them sound and practical advice to solve their problems. But off late, he had taken to simply saying that all problems that occurred were for their own good! They could not understand the logic underlying his words. But their faith in him was implicit and absolute, and they were content to obey him.

The following day, the entire village, men, women and children, rushed out to meet him early in the morning. All the fires in the village houses had got put out overnight. In those days, there were no matchsticks, and lighting fires was a difficult task. Villagers would keep the fires burning in their huts simply by covering them partially; a few sparks would help them rekindle the fires the following day. But now that every fire had died out, nobody could cook any food!

The seer spent a long time in meditation before addressing the villagers, 'Believe me when I tell you, this too, is for your own good. Go home peacefully now. We cannot cook any food today, but an occasional fast will not do us any harm.'

The villagers were completely mystified. The younger ones mumbled, 'It's alright for him, as he is a renunciate. But we are the ones who will find it difficult to fast!'

Later that day, an unforeseen event occurred. The region was invaded by marauding tribes from across the border, and the chieftain of the tribes had a single goal: To loot, kill and destroy all the people and their villages. The armies of the invaders marched by on the opposite bank of the river, identifying villages from afar by the smoke arising from the chimneys and the sound of dogs barking or cocks crowing. The raiders would then swoop down on the unsuspecting villagers, loot, plunder and kill, and leave as quickly as they had arrived. The villagers could hear the click of galloping horse hooves, and the terrible battle cries of the marauders. They shook with fear. But the armies passed them by completely. No smoke could be seen, there were no dogs to bark and no cocks to crow. The invading chieftain ordered his soldiers to ride on to the next village, for this village, as he could see, was obviously uninhabited. And the villagers had a lucky escape!

They rushed to the ascetic and fell at his feet, tears of gratitude flowing from their eyes. He blessed them and said, 'Dear brothers and sisters, there is a meaning of mercy in all that happens to us. When the Lord abides in our hearts, we have nothing to fear.'

Understanding

A student asked his Zen master why the Japanese make their teacups so thin and delicate that they break easily. 'It's not that they're too delicate,' replied the master. 'But that they require delicate and correct handling, which many people are not capable of. You must learn the art of handling difficult and delicate situations. It is you who must adjust yourself to the environment and not vice versa.'

WARMING UP

Today, cultivate the spirit of silent acceptance of God's Will. Things always don't happen the way we want them to; things do not always work out to our complete satisfaction. Today, bear silent witness to such negative trends, and let them pass. Do not fret, become impatient or annoyed. Instead, utter a silent prayer of acceptance and convince yourself, 'Whatever the Lord Wills, must be for my own good.' You will feel a tremendous sense of peace and joy descend into your heart.

Words of Wisdom

Adversities strengthen the mind as labour does the body.

—*Seneca*

I know God will not give me anything I can't handle. I just wish that He didn't trust me so much.

—*Mother Teresa*

Life's challenges are not supposed to paralyse you, they're supposed to help you discover who you are.

—*Bernice Johnson Reagon*

Difficulties are God's errands, and when we are sent upon them we should esteem it a proof of God's confidence—as a compliment from Him.

—*HW Beecher*

Lesson 11

Forgive and Forget

Life is too short to be spent in fault-finding, holding grudges or keeping memory of wrongs done to us. Forgive even before forgiveness is asked for. Forgive and forget.

The following story was narrated by Gautama Buddha to stop two warring princes from destroying each other.

Brahmadatta was the king of Benaras. When he conquered his neighbouring kingdom, Kaushala, he sought to kill Dirgheti, the king of that country and his queen, so that his rule would be secure. However, Dirgheti and his wife made good their escape. They went into hiding and lived in disguise at the humble dwelling of a potter who was their loyal and devout follower.

In time, they had a son called Dirghayu whom they brought up with loving care. When he was sixteen, he was sent to a *gurukul* to complete his education.

When the son was away, Dirgheti and his queen were spotted by a barber who recognised them and betrayed their secret hiding place to Brahmadatta. Determined to destroy his old enemy, Brahmadatta ordered that they be executed.

A large crowd gathered to witness the execution in Benaras. Among the crowd was Dirghayu, who was shocked and grieved to find that his parents were about to be killed. However, Dirgheti saw him pushing his way through the crowds and gave him a warning shout, 'Oh my son, do not look long, do not look short. Hatred is not appeased by hatred, but by non-hatred alone.'

That stopped Dirghayu in his tracks, for he realised the wisdom of his father's words. Brahmadatta realised that there was a son somewhere in the crowd, but there was no way he could spot him. Then, before the eyes of their son, King Dirgheti and his wife were executed. Dirghayu was devastated. He was left with a terrible sense of loss and pain.

Years rolled by. Dirghayu became an expert elephant handler and found employment in the royal elephant stables. Here, he would play the flute when he was free. One day, the king heard him play and was enchanted by its melody. He summoned the flute player. Suitably impressed by the young man, who appeared handsome, virtuous and courteous, the king appointed him as his chosen companion and confidante, the one who would accompany him wherever he went.

Little did Brahmadatta realise that this young man whom he held in such affection and trust was the son of the king whom he had executed so ruthlessly. Nor did he know that Dirghayu was just biding his time, looking for the right opportunity to kill him and seek revenge.

One fine day, that long-awaited opportunity came knocking. During a forest hunt, Brahmadatta and Dirghayu got separated from the rest of the king's party, as they went chasing their quarry. Dirghayu was driving the king's chariot. They stopped when they realised they had lost the others, and got down from the chariot. It was a hot day and the king was tired. Dirghayu asked him to lay his head on his lap and go to sleep. The king did so without hesitation as he trusted the young man absolutely.

Soon he was fast asleep. Dirghayu saw that this was the opportunity he had been waiting for all along. There was no one around, and the king was utterly in his power. Quietly, the young man unsheathed his sword. But then, the words of his father echoed in his mind and he had to put the sword away.

At the same time, the king was awakened by a terrible nightmare. He dreamt that the son of the royal couple executed by him, had managed to reach him, and was standing over him with a drawn sword, ready to kill him in vengeance.

As the king narrated this frightening dream, Dirghayu drew his sword again and said, 'That was no ordinary dream. It was a warning to you. I am the son you dreamt of, and I am about to kill you to avenge the death of my parents.'

'Please spare my life!' begged the king, holding the young man's hands in despair. 'Do not kill me, I beg of you.'

'Surely O King, you will have me executed if I spare your life,' countered Dirghayu. 'For you know my identity now, and you will not have me around, as I am the royal heir to the throne of Kaushala. If I don't kill you, I must get killed!'

'Let us then make a pact not to kill each other,' suggested the king. 'Let this vicious cycle of fear, hatred and vindictiveness be broken forever!'

The two then pledged lifelong loyalty and friendship. The king, once he recovered from his traumatic experience, asked Dirghayu to tell him the meaning of his father's intriguing final message.

Dirghayu explained to him, 'Do not look long—it means do not nurse your hatred for a long time. Do not look short—this means do not act hastily. If I had acted hastily, I would have killed you, only to be killed by your guards when they found us. Then my friends and followers would pursue your people in vengeance and the hatred will continue. However, you and I have extended mutual forgiveness, and therefore both of us can be free of fear. The cycle of violence is now broken.'

Concluding the story, Buddha reminded his disciples that hatred only leads to further hatred, while love and forgiveness can conquer hatred and promote peace.

UNDERSTANDING

Each day is like a blank page that you fill with your thoughts, words and deeds. If you want a beautiful page, be aware of your thoughts and strive to be the best you can be. But, if you do make mistakes, admit them and forgive yourself. You are here to grow and God does not expect you to be perfect all the time. Just learn from the mistakes and you will grow!

Many of us are ready to practise the virtue of forgiveness on others, but it is equally important to forgive oneself and forget what God wishes us to forget.

Warming Up

Make slips of paper. On each slip, write the name of a person or mention an incident that you are unable to forgive or forget. These people and incidents must relate to your 'bad' memories, which you are unable to wipe away from your consciousness, and which have left you with long-lasting wounds.

When you are sure that all bad memories have been listed, sit in front of a candle or a flame of a lamp and burn away each slip of paper, and along with it, each one of those painful memories. As each slip is burnt, say to yourself loudly, 'I let go of this memory, and now I am free of its pain and negativity!'

Words of Wisdom

Those who are free of resentful thoughts surely find peace.

—*Gautama Buddha*

The weak can never forgive. Forgiveness is the
attribute of the strong.

—*Mahatma Gandhi*

To be angry is to let others' mistakes punish yourself.
To forgive others is to be good to yourself.

—*Master Cheng Yen*

Forgiveness is the fragrance that the violet sheds
on the heel that has crushed it.

—*Mark Twain*

He who cannot forgive breaks the bridge over
which he himself must pass.

—*George Herbert*

Lesson 12

Worst Thing

The worst thing that can happen to a man is that he has a hot head and a cold heart.

Thirteen-year-old Raju was enjoying an early morning walk with his father by the seashore. Bandstand was as yet uncrowded; it was too early for the usual rush of joggers and strollers. Mr Gupta and Raju were walking briskly, exhilarated by the freshness of the sea breeze and the gentle rays of the morning sun. Unobstructed by other walkers, they took large strides, feeling as if the entire stretch of Bandstand was reserved exclusively for their use.

'I'll tell you what, Papa,' Raju said to his father excitedly, 'I'll race you to the end of the promenade. One...two...let's go!'

Father and son began their race, both of them laughing, and also, challenging each other. In his eagerness to beat his father, Raju had already taken an early lead, when his father's voice called out to him urgently, 'Stop, Raju, stop! Turn back at once! We are returning home.'

'Papa, that's not fair,' Raju cried, a bit out of breath, but bitterly disappointed. 'It's not even six o'clock yet! Why should we return home so early?'

But Mr Gupta had already turned around, and was walking away from the promenade. Puzzled, Raju turned to look back at the track they had quit, and then realisation dawned. 'Wait, Papa, wait,' he called out reaching Mr Gupta's side and hooked his arm through his father's. 'I know why you turned back,' he whispered connivingly. 'It's that nasty man, Mr Das, isn't it?'

'Watch your language, Raju,' warned his father. 'Don't refer to elders so disrespectfully.'

'Sorry, Papa, but I do think he is nasty. Why, he has borrowed money from you, and you are the one who feels embarrassed to confront him and ask him to return it! The way we are hurrying away from this place, anyone would think, it was you who borrowed money from him, and are now scared to face him. And look at him, he just doesn't care, does he? He keeps making some excuse or the other, and slips away.'

'That's not true, Raju,' corrected his father sternly. 'Mr Das is a very elderly gentleman, and a friend of my father's. He took a loan from me and promised to return it within a year. It's been five years, and he has not been able to keep his word. Poor man! He is so embarrassed to see me that I simply don't want to cross his path. I have never once asked him to return the money, but he has told me several times that he is going to borrow money from a family member and return my money. I really do not wish to put him through any further humiliation or trouble on account of this loan.'

'If you're so sensitive about it, Papa, why don't you simply tell him that he can keep the money as a gift, and that you don't want it back from him?'

'As a matter of fact, that's exactly what I told him when I ran into him last week at the bank.'

'He must have been mighty pleased to hear that,' put in Raju sarcastically. 'He accepted your offer, didn't he?'

'As a matter of fact, he did not,' Mr. Gupta replied with a smile. 'He felt quite insulted. He told me he was not a beggar, and had no intention of accepting charity from me or from any of his friends.'

'Well!' exclaimed Raju in surprise, 'Now who would have thought he would bowl a googly like that? But why are you running away from him now?'

'He is sure to feel uncomfortable on seeing me now, and will again offer to repay the amount. As for me, I have no wish to put him in a tight spot. So I prefer to avoid meeting him face to face right now.'

'Papa, you know what?' said Raju, his eyes shining. 'I think you're really the perfect gentleman, the white knight in shining armour that our English teacher talks about! It is usually the borrower who hesitates to meet the lender. In your case, it is the opposite. I'm proud of you, Papa! Do you think I'll be like you, when I grow up?'

Mr Gupta only smiled as he led Raju away from the promenade.

UNDERSTANDING

What is your SQ—Spiritual Quotient? Here, is a simple test that you can take:

Q1. Your friend forgets to call you on your birthday. How do you react?

1. I freak out.

2. I understand, but I am still annoyed.

3. I telephone my friend and with a smile say, 'Hey, it's my birthday today. And it won't be complete without you wishing me. So please give me your good wishes.'

Q2. You are overloaded with work at the office. Your spouse complains that you have no time for her and your mother has to be admitted in the hospital for a few tests. What would you do?

1. I would be a wreck.

2. I would recognise that I am being pulled in all directions, but still be unable to say no to anyone.

3. I will draw firm boundaries, maintain my work and personal time, and yet, put forth my best efforts.

Q3. At a time of great suffering:

1. I go into a downward spiral.

2. I care for myself and for others, trying not to add to anyone's suffering.

3. I accept this as part of the human experience, and see it as an opportunity for spiritual growth.

If most of your answers were the third option, you are quite an evolved person spiritually! If you chose mostly the second option, you have come a long way, but still have a long way to go.

If your answers were the first option, your spiritual quotient is currently low, but it is never too late to begin!

Warming Up

Do you wish to develop a warm heart? There is a simple way to achieve this. Put yourself in the other person's shoes. Try to see the events and happenings of the day from another's point of view. Feel their pains and sorrows and forget yourself for the time being.

You will soon realise how cold-hearted and indifferent we are otherwise!

Words of Wisdom

Holding on to anger is like grasping a hot coal
with the intent of throwing it at someone else;
you are the one who gets burned.

—*Gautama Buddha*

For every minute you remain angry, you give up
sixty seconds of peace of mind.

—*Ralph Waldo Emerson*

Every time you get angry, you poison your own system.

—*Alfred Montapert*

When angry, count to ten before you speak; if very
angry, a hundred.

—*Thomas Jefferson*

Lesson 13

The Past Does Not Bind Us

If a person has moved in the wrong direction, he can always make a U-turn. The Angels of God will be with him. The past does not—cannot—bind us!

Buddha was in a village congregation, telling the assembled people about the power of *maitri* and compassion. A fierce looking man walked past the gathering and stood before the master. To the utter shock and confusion of the disciples surrounding Buddha, he spat on Buddha's snow-white stole.

Calmly, the master wiped away the filthy saliva stain from his garment, and said to the man, 'Thank you for that, my friend. Have you anything more to say to me?'

Nonplussed, the man moved away, not looking back or having a word in reply.

'Master! That man's act was dastardly!' cried Ananda, who was one of the many shocked spectators. 'Why did you speak to him so politely? He deserved to be thrashed!'

'My dear Ananda, words can never express all that we feel,' the master explained. 'Language always falls short of strong feelings. When we are overcome with love and affection, we find it easier to give the other person a hug, rather than trying to tell him what we feel about him. So it is with wrath. When we are too angry for words, our indignation finds expression in a gesture like the one made by our friend. I was concerned that the violent outburst would still have left him seething. That is why I asked him if he had managed to vent out all of his anger, or had something left to express against me.'

The following day, Buddha left the village to travel to the next stop in his wanderings. But the angry man was left feeling guilty and ashamed after his outburst. He followed the saint to the next village, hiding himself away till the congregation dispersed after the master's discourse. Under the cover of darkness, he approached the master yet again. Not to be caught napping this time, the disciples drew near the master, who silently gestured them to remain where they were. The man drew near and fell at Buddha's feet, weeping, shedding bitter tears of sorrow and repentance.

'Forgive me, O Compassionate One,' he sobbed. 'I am ashamed of myself! I can never live down the ignominy of my shameful conduct yesterday. I carry a heavy burden in my heart. Do thou forgive me?'

'Yesterday?!' exclaimed the Buddha. 'So much water has flown down the Ganga since yesterday, and you still dwell there? Today is a new day, my friend.'

'True, it is another time, another day,' agreed the man. 'Nevertheless, I beg you to forgive me.'

'Go in peace,' the master said to him, 'let life flow on like the waters of the Ganga. Let the past remain behind. Live for now, and forget what happened yesterday.'

Understanding

How to make a U-turn in life?

1. First and foremost, you should realise that you have wasted all your years in wandering—in moving away from your goal. Every passing day has taken you farther and farther away from the goal that, for want of a better word, we call God. It is time to make a U-turn.

2. Prepare yourself. Switch on the indicator signal that shows the direction of your turn.

3. Check for oncoming traffic. Block all negative thoughts that discourage you from making the turn.

4. Press the accelerator ever so lightly. Seek help and inspiration from God who supplies the required strength when you need.

5. Steer the wheel of your life towards the destination you have chosen.

6. Enter your new lane and keep driving forward!

WARMING UP

Today, reserve your special thoughts and prayers for all who have lost their way in the journey of life. Ask God to help them; send them your positive thoughts. For prayer is a potent and powerful way to help us make a U-turn back to God!

Words of Wisdom

Do not dwell in the past; do not dream of the future, concentrate the mind on the present moment.

—*Gautama Buddha*

Though no one can go back and make a brand new start, anyone can start from now and make a brand new ending.

—*Carl Bard*

Lesson 14

MIRACLES OF GOD

You, who are looking for miracles, open your eyes and see! All around us are the miracles of God. A tiny seed grows into a huge banyan tree. A caterpillar becomes a butterfly.

We all have heard of the famous parable of the 'sower and the seed' from the Bible. But one of the non-canonical versions of the New Testament also contains the parable of the 'growing seed'. Let me share it with you:

He said, 'The Kingdom of God is as if a man should cast seed on the earth, and should sleep and rise night and day, and the seed should spring up and grow, he doesn't know how. For the earth bears fruit—first the blade, then the ear, then the full grain in the ear. But when the fruit is ripe, immediately he puts forth the sickle, because the harvest has come.'

I was reminded of this parable when a friend sent me the following story. It is credited to Novoneel Chakraborty, and since it is written so beautifully and simply, I give it to you verbatim:

Once upon a time, there was a seed and because it was only a seed, nobody cared to notice it. Thus, gripped by a sense of inferiority, the seed gave no importance to its existence. Then one day, a wind picked it up, randomly or otherwise, it did not know, and threw it mercilessly on an open field under the sweltering sun. The seed lay confused. Why would one do such a thing? But instead of getting any answers, it was drenched with rain, sometimes in drizzles and sometimes in torrents. It was bathed in sunlight too.

Meanwhile, time flew. One day, a traveller came and sat beside the seed.

'Thank You God for this,' it heard the traveller say. 'I really needed some rest.'

'What are you talking about?' the seed promptly asked. For it thought the man was surely mocking it. The seed had seen many people sit beside it, more so in recent years, but no one ever spoke like that.

'Who is this?' countered the man, startled by the seed's question.

'This is me, the seed.'

'The seed?' the man looked at the giant tree. 'Are you kidding me? You are no seed. You are a tree. A goliath of a tree!'

'Really?'

'Yes! Why else do you think people come here?'

'I don't know. What do they come here for?'

'To luxuriate in your shade! Don't tell me you didn't know you had grown over time.'

A moment passed before the traveller's words struck the chord of realisation in the seed.

The seed, which was now a beautiful, spreading tree, thought awhile, and smiled for the first time in its life. The years of relentless torture under the sun and the rain, finally made sense.

'Oh! That means I'm not a tiny, flimsy seed anymore! I wasn't destined to die unnoticed, but was actually born to relieve people of their weariness. Wow! Now that's a life worth living!'

Understanding

Look around with a new, fresh vision. Notice the trees and plants and creepers, which you tend to take for granted. Were they always there? Have you witnessed the miracle of their growth?

Express your gratitude to God for the miracle of creation—for the blue sky, the life-giving warmth of the sun, the enchanting silvery light of the moon, the myriad stars, the birds, the flowers, the grass, the butterflies and all that, which makes up the unparalleled beauty of creation!

Warming Up

Make a list of simple miracles that you see, but have never had the time to pay attention to. It could be anything—the simple fact that the sun rises with precision everyday, the birds that know exactly where to fly this season or the hidden intelligence in every aspect of nature.

Words of Wisdom

To look out at this kind of creation out here and not believe in God is to me impossible. It just strengthens my faith. I wish there were words to describe what it's like.

—*John Glenn*

While I know myself as a creation of God, I am also obligated to realise and remember that everyone else and everything else are also God's creation.

—*Maya Angelou*

The creation of a thousand forests is in one acorn.

—*Ralph Waldo Emerson*

Lesson 15

LOVE IS THE POWER

Open thine heart and let love enter in—and all things in the universe will gravitate to thee.

For love is the power that pulls.

Once upon a time, there lived a magnificent and rare white elephant, who was an extremely kind-hearted soul. He loved his mother who had grown blind and feeble and could not look after herself. So he left his herd, and took her to Mount Candorana to live in a cave beside a beautiful lake that was covered by gorgeous pink lotuses. His only joy in life was to pick the most delicious fruits and the most delicate and sweet stems and offer them to his mother. If she had looked after him and fed him lovingly in childhood, now it was he who took on the role of a loving son and guardian in her blind and helpless condition.

One day, a forester who was roaming the hills spotted him. At first, he was terrified of the huge creature, for he felt that it might stamp him under his foot. He ran as fast as his legs could carry him, and fell headlong into a ditch. It was the kind elephant who rescued him, told him not to be afraid, and carried him on his back to the edge of the forest. The man thanked him profoundly and made his way to the city of Benaras.

Upon reaching the city, he heard that King Brahmadatta's personal elephant had just died and the king was looking for a new elephant. His heralds were roaming the city, announcing that any man who had seen or heard of an elephant fit for a king, should come forward with the information. He would be richly rewarded.

The forester was very excited and immediately went up to the king and recounted seeing the white elephant on Mount Candorana. He said that he had marked the way, but would require the help of a couple of elephant trainers to snare this fantastic elephant.

The king was thrilled with this information and immediately dispatched a number of soldiers and elephant trainers along with the forester. After crossing much of the forest, the group reached the lake beside which the elephants lived. The men slowly crept down to the edge of the lake and hid behind the bushes. The white elephant was collecting lotus shoots for his mother's meal and immediately sensed the presence of humans. When he looked up, he spotted the forester and realised that he was the one who had led the king's men to him. The elephant was deeply hurt by the man's ingratitude, but deduced that if he put up a struggle, many of the men would be killed. And he was just too kind to hurt anyone. So he decided to go along with them to Benaras and then request the benevolent king to set him free.

That night when the white elephant did not return home, his mother was very worried. She had heard all the commotion outside and guessed that the king's men had probably taken away her son. She was scared that the king would ride him into battle and her son would definitely be killed. She was also worried that there would be no one to look after her or even feed her, as she could not see. So she just lay down and cried bitterly.

Meanwhile, her son was led into the beautiful city of Benaras, where he was given a grand reception. The whole city was decorated and his own stable was gaily painted and covered with garlands of fragrant flowers. The trainers laid out a feast for their new state elephant, but he refused to touch a morsel. He remained unresponsive to every effort. The fragrant flowers, the beautiful and comfortable stable left him unmoved. He just sat there, looking completely despondent.

The worried trainers rushed to report the strange situation to their king. They were scared the elephant would simply waste away if it did not take any food or water. The king grew extremely concerned when he heard this and went to the stable himself to investigate. He offered the elephant food from the royal table and asked him why he was grieving in this manner. He suggested that the elephant should feel proud and honoured as he had been chosen as the state elephant and would get the opportunity to serve his king.

But the white elephant replied that he would not eat a thing until he met his mother. The king then enquired about the whereabouts of his mother. The elephant replied that she was waiting back home on Mount Candorana, and must be worried and hungry, as she was blind and had no one to feed her and take care of her. He was afraid that she would die.

The compassionate king was touched by the elephant's story and asked him to return to his blind, old mother and take care of her as he had been doing all along. He set him free in a display of love and kindness.

The happy elephant scampered back home as fast as he could. He was so relieved to find that his mother was still alive. He filled his trunk with water and poured it over his sick mother, who thought that it must be raining. Then she cried out as she thought some evil spirit had come to harm her, and wished and prayed that her son was there to save her.

The white elephant gently bent over his blind mother and stroked her lovingly. She recognised his touch instantly and was overjoyed. Her son then lifted her up and recounted how the kind and compassionate king of Benaras had set him free so that he could return to love and look after his mother forever.

The relieved and ecstatic mother blessed the kind king, wishing him much peace, prosperity and joy till the end of his days. She profusely expressed her thanks to him for sending her son back home.

The white elephant stayed with his mother and took good care of her till the day she died. And when he died himself, the king erected a statue of him beside the lake, and held an annual elephant festival there in memory of the caring and noble soul.

Understanding

True love is unselfish. It gives without ever expecting anything in return. The love that looks for reward and compensation is barter, it is trade. Not me, but you—that's the attitude of true love.

'Not me, but you'—this is the motto of the National Service Scheme, which was started to inculcate in the youth of India, a sense of dedication and social commitment towards the society and its people, especially the downtrodden.

Not me, but you—how beautiful the world would be, if all of us adopt this as our motto!

We could try practising it for at least one day at a time! Just for today, let us learn to put others first. Let our selfish needs and wants take a back seat. Let us look to offer others the help they need. When we practise this, we are practising genuine love!

Warming Up

If we wish to let love enter our hearts, we have to seek the source of love. The source of all love is God; He is the universal powerhouse of love! So today, let us turn to Him, again and again, and beg Him to shower His love upon us. He is true and unconditional in His love.

Words of Wisdom

Love is a fruit in season at all times, and within reach of every hand.

—*Mother Teresa*

All love is expansion, all selfishness is contraction. Love is therefore the only law of life. He who loves lives, he who is selfish is dying. Therefore, love for love's sake, because it is the law of life, just as you breathe to live.

—*Swami Vivekanada*

The most important thing in life is to learn how to give out love, and to let it come in.

—*Morrie Schwartz*

I have found the paradox that if I love until it hurts, then there is no hurt, but only more love.

—*Mother Teresa*

Lesson 16

GIVE, GIVE, GIVE!

Give, give, give—until it hurts to give! This will release you from bondage to the ego and to things.

It is narrated from Imam Musa Kadhim, that in Bani Israel lived a righteous man, who had a kind-hearted wife.

One night, this man had a dream in which someone told him that the Almighty Allah had fixed a particular life chart for him. Half of his life was to be in prosperity, and the other half in difficulties. He was given the choice whichever phase of life he desired, he could have first, and then fulfil the remaining condition later in life. The man requested for some time as he wanted to consult his wife, for he had always sought her counsel in important matters.

The next day, he related this dream to his wife who told him to seek the prosperous phase of life first. She said, 'And hurry up to obtain it. Maybe, Almighty Allah wishes to grant us with His bounties.' The next night, when he was asked about his choice in his dream, the man wished for prosperity in the early half of life. His wish shall be fulfilled, he was reassured.

And soon, he began to receive abundant rewards that turned life comfortable. His wealth and property increased.

Then his wife said, 'O slave of Almighty Allah! Now, you help your relatives and other deprived people. Do good to them. Give that particular thing to that neighbour, and something to that friend of yours.'

The man followed the advice of his wife and generously gave away much of his wealth in charity. In this way, half his life passed. And then again, he dreamt of the same person, who now had this to say, 'You were not stingy in charity, therefore the Almighty Allah has decided to grant you prosperity in the latter half of your life also.'

Understanding

Today, make it your day to care and share!

Share your smiles with everyone you meet. Share some of your food with the less fortunate ones. Offer a share of your day's spending in charity, and go without something you want.

Warming Up

What is your most prized possession? Gold? Jewellery? Your expensive wristwatch or sunglasses?

If there is one personal belonging that you are very attached to and feel proud to own, close your eyes and visualise that you are giving it away to a very needy person who is ecstatic to receive it. Watch the resistance of the mind. Become aware of the selfishness arising from our attachments. This is the first step towards realising that we need to give, give and give, yet again!

Words of Wisdom

Allah (SWT), the Wise, has said
in the Noble Qur'an:

Give to your close relatives what they need, and also give generously to the destitute and to wayfarers. Do not squander your wealth; those who are wasteful are the brothers and sisters of Satan and Satan is always ungrateful to his Lord. But if, while waiting for the Lord's bounty, you are unable to help your relatives, the destitute and wayfarers, then at least speak kindly to them.

—*Surah Al-Isra*

We make a living with what we get, but we make a life with what we give.

—*Winston Churchill*

Lesson 17

We Cannot Deceive Nature

I must never forget that every thought I think; every word I utter; every action I perform; every feeling, every emotion that wakes up within me, is recorded in the memory of nature.

I may be able to deceive those around me. I may even succeed in deceiving myself. But I cannot deceive nature.

Little Mohan was returning home from the Sadhu Vaswani *gurukul* classes. As he turned into the quiet tree-lined lane where his house stood, he was singing loudly the song he had learnt in the *gurukul* class that day. He stopped to pick up a stone and examine it closely; he plucked a leaf to lift the caterpillar that was crawling on the pavement, and put it on the grass verge; he peered into a fluffy-winged seed before blowing it away into the air. He climbed a little tree in the neighbour's garden to peer into a nest and ensure that the younglings of the sparrow were safe inside, and all this while, he kept singing cheerfully.

His neighbour called out to the boy from the open window, 'Where have you been, Mohan? And what's all the singing about?'

'I went to my Sunday *gurukul* classes,' chirped Mohan. 'And the song is about God, don't you know?'

'So what did they teach you at the *gurukul* classes?'

'That God is with us, He is watching us and watching over us all the time.'

'I'll tell you what, my little boy,' said the neighbour, 'show me where God is, and I'll give you a brand new ten-rupee note.'

Little Mohan tilted his head thoughtfully and considered the attractive offer made to him. Then he looked up and said to the neighbour, 'And I'll tell you what, Mr Gurudutt. You show me where God is *not*, and I'll tell my father to give you a brand new five-hundred-rupee note!'

Understanding

The children were lined up in the cafeteria of an elementary school for lunch. At the head of the table, stood a large pile of apples. The teacher wrote a note and posted it on the apple tray, 'Take only one. God is watching.'

Moving further along the lunch line, at the other end of the table, lay a large pile of chocolate chip cookies. One child whispered to another, 'Take all you want. God is watching the apples.'

Many of us tend to be like this child. We think God is not watching, listening, all the time and all the things. He may be unaware of some words, actions and thoughts, we may think. But God is aware of every idea, every impulse, every thought that flashes even for an instant across our consciousness.

Let us be a little more mature than the child in the story. Let us remember, God is watching the cookies too!

Warming Up

Today, practise the presence of God in your life. Try and retain the awareness that He is with you, watching you and watching over you. Let your words and actions reveal this awareness. Would you dare to rebuke your subordinate so harshly if God was within earshot? Would you indulge in malicious gossip and complaints if He were part of your group? Would you turn away a beggar rudely or ignore a needy person, if you knew He was watching you?

See what this awareness does to you as you get on with your routine daily activities.

Words of Wisdom

The limitless nature and the omnipresent God
are indistinguishable from each other.

—*Atharva Veda*

The eyes of the Lord are in every place,
beholding the evil and the good!

—*Proverbs 15:3*

Steadfastness in knowledge of the Supreme Spirit, and the perception of [the omnipresent God as] the object of true knowledge is called knowledge; what is contrary to this, is ignorance.

—*Srimad Bhagavad Gita*

Nature is too thin a screen; the glory of the omnipresent God bursts through everywhere.

—*Ralph Waldo Emerson*

Lesson 18

LET GO, LET GOD!

When a particular problem has vexed you for sometime and you are unable to do anything about it, hand it over to God.

Breathe out the aspiration, 'Thy Will be done, O Lord!'

Soon, a way will be shown to you.

A small and devout group of villagers living in an obscure hamlet in the foothills of the Great Smoky Mountains, USA decided to build a new church on a piece of land that had been left to them by a church member in his will.

Ten days before the opening of the new church, the local building inspector informed the vicar that the new church did not conform to the state building regulations as its parking lot was inadequate for the size of the building. Until the church doubled the size of the parking lot, he could not give clearance to use the new building.

Unfortunately, the new church with its small parking lot had used every inch of the land bequeathed in the will, except for the hillock against which it had been built. In order to build more parking spaces, they would have to move the 'mountain' out of their backyard.

Undaunted, the pastor announced the next Sunday morning that he would meet that evening with all members who had 'mountain-moving faith'. They would hold a prayer session asking God to remove the mountain from their backyard, and to somehow provide enough money to have it paved and painted, so that the official sanction to use the building could be obtained from the county sheriff before the opening dedication service, scheduled for the following week.

At the appointed time, twenty-four of the 300 congregation members assembled for prayer. They prayed for nearly three hours. At ten o'clock the pastor finally said, 'Amen'.

'We'll open next Sunday as scheduled,' he assured everyone. 'God has never let us down before, and I believe He will protect the faithful this time too.'

The next morning, as he was working in his study there was a loud knock at his door. When he called, 'Come in', a rough-looking construction foreman appeared, removing his hard hat as he entered.

'Excuse me, Reverend. I'm from Acme Construction Company, over in the next county. We're building a huge new shopping mall over there and need some fill dirt. According to county records, your church owns the little hillock behind your parking lot. Would you be willing to sell us a chunk of that hillock behind the church? We'll pay you for the dirt we remove and pave all the exposed area free of charge, if you let us have it right away. Our bulldozers are ready to move in the moment you give us the go ahead. You see, we can't do any work on our building site until we get the dirt in and allow it to settle properly.'

The little church was opened the next Sunday as originally planned and there were far more members with 'mountain-moving faith' on opening Sunday than there had been the previous week.

Understanding

Most of us are faithful believers. We have our 'good' days when we have strong faith in ourselves and we feel that God is with us. There is a sense of purpose and clarity in all that we do, we know where we are heading and we act with confidence, doors seem to open effortlessly and we are 'with the flow' as it were.

But we also pass through periods when we have to struggle against feelings of fear, self-doubt, insecurity and disorientation of purpose. Fear and faith cannot coexist together, and when fear is stronger, faith recedes.

The way out through this situation is to stay with faith so that our lives and hearts are filled with the light of faith. Here are a few tips that can help you:

1. Accept yourself as you are, with all your weaknesses and limitations. An exaggerated ego is not the same as self-confidence.

2. Think positively. Use affirmations to boost your self-confidence. Visualise yourself succeeding through hard work and faith.

3. Think of the solution, not of the problem. Look at the situation

before you, as you would be looking at a jigsaw puzzle in which you have to fit the next piece you are carrying.

4. Spend some time in silent meditation, looking for guidance and answers to your questions from within.

Warming Up

Today, meditate on this mantra: I will walk with God today, and trust Him for tomorrow.

Words of Wisdom

Setting aside all noble deeds, just surrender
completely to the Will of God. I shall liberate
you from all sins. Do not grieve.

—*Srimad Bhagavad Gita*

One of the most arduous spiritual tasks is that of
giving up control and allowing the Spirit of God
to lead our lives.

—*Henri Nouwen*

Lesson 19

Work or Love

Does God want our work? Or does He want our love?

He wants that we should work for Him in love.

Ambadas was a devoted disciple of Samarth Ramdas, one of the great gurus of Maharashtra. Ambadas served the guru with great devotion and obedience. But in his heart burned a deep desire to have the darshan of Sri Rama, his *ishta devata*. Ambadas knew only his guru could help him achieve his heart's desire.

Are not God and guru the same? The guru, without being told, knew of his disciple's deep longing and decided to grant his desire. He also thought it would be an example for his other disciples, teaching them how important it is to be devoted to your guru.

One day, as Samarth Ramdas and his disciples were resting under the shade of a tree, the guru's eyes fell on a branch of the tree that overhung a deep, abandoned well. He called Ambadas and said, 'I want you to climb on this overhanging branch, sit on its edge and cut it off from the trunk of the tree. Do not sit close to the trunk, sit on the branch, face the trunk and cut the branch off.'

With alacrity, Ambadas sprang up to do his guru's bidding. Within minutes, he was happily chopping away at the branch, unmindful of his precarious position, perched above the deep well on the very edge of the branch he was cutting off. If he was aware that he would fall into the well with the chopped branch, he certainly did not show it. As for the other disciples, they grinned and sniggered at what they thought was his sheer foolishness. They believed the guru would demonstrate to them what a *murkha*—idiot—Ambadas was, and urge them to be wiser and more discriminating.

Things occurred just as they had expected. The branch broke away from the trunk and fell into the deep well with a great clutter. Now, the disciples thought, surely the guru would rush to help Ambadas for he had fallen into the well along with the branch.

But the guru did no such thing. He continued to rest in peace. The disciples first went numb in shock and fear, then opened their mouths to point out the fate of poor Ambadas.

'Sir, what has become of Ambadas?' they demanded fearfully. 'Should we not go to his rescue?'

'Let us ask Ambadas himself,' replied the guru, calmly. Loudly, he called out to his fallen disciple. 'Ambadas! Ambadas! How are you? What is your state now?'

An excited voice answered from the depth of the well, 'O Gurudev! I am in the seventh heaven! I have no words to praise your grace and power!'

The guru had so ordained that when Ambadas fell into the well, he would land in the arms of the Divine Lord, Sri Rama, whose darshan he had sought with such yearning and devotion. Carrying out the guru's order with implicit obedience, Ambadas had got what he wanted—darshan of his *ishta devta*.

The disciples rushed to peer into the well and were stunned by the sight that met their eyes! They learnt that day an unforgettable lesson on the value of obedience!

The guru does not need outer acts of reverence from you. What matters to him most is your inner attitude of reverence and devotion in acts of obedience. For this culminates in self-realisation.

Understanding

How can we turn work into worship? The answer is very simple. Whatever you do, do it as an offering to God. Whatever the nature of your work, do it for the love of God. Your work will then be truly blessed.

Have you heard of the distinguished visitor who visited a quarry to talk to the poor labourers who were toiling hard, breaking stones? He walked up to some of the men working there and asked each the same question, 'What are you doing?'

The first one snarled angrily, 'Can't you see, I am breaking stones?'

The second one wiped the sweat off his brow and replied, 'I am earning a living to feed my wife and children.'

The third man looked up at him and said cheerfully, 'I am helping build a beautiful temple!'

Now, you know who out of the three men had managed to turn his work into a form of worship and created good karma for himself, although all of them were doing the same job!

Warming Up

Many of us work for a living. Work has become an intrinsic part of our lives today, and we treat it as a matter of routine. But we must become aware that it is our thought and intention that determine the kind of karma we create for ourselves through work. Therefore, we must learn to be aware of the motivation, the impulse that leads us to act or speak in a particular manner. Very often, we are not conscious of our intentions, and this may set up a bad karmic environment.

As we become conscious of our intentions, especially those that motivate us to act, we become better aware of the karma we are creating for ourselves. And when we are aware and vigilant, the fruit of our actions are manifest to us. We become conscious of the law of cause and effect, and we can clearly perceive when our actions are motivated by hatred or jealousy, for they inevitably inflict suffering upon us. On the other hand, when we are motivated by love, goodwill or compassion, our actions bring joy to us and others. Thus we realise, when we pay attention to our thoughts and intentions, which serve as motivating forces, we are actually shaping our everyday lives.

Each of us can promote good karma in our day-to-day life, simply by performing acts of goodness, kindness, compassion and love. We must endeavour in every possible way to serve God in humanity and indeed, in all creation. All actions that are born out of goodwill, understanding, compassion and selflessness are good karma. When you perform such actions, they usher in peace and joy.

I know quite a few people who complain that they don't get time to eat during the day. I do believe them! They go through endless cups of coffee and tea, skipping breakfast or lunch. Maybe, they 'grab a sandwich' while they are working, but that's about all.

Today, stop to ask yourself, 'Why is this happening to me? Is there anything I can do about it? Can I possibly take control of my life and slow down the pace so that I am aware of the present?'

Let us cultivate greater awareness, so that we live in the present, and enjoy everything that we do—whether it is drinking tea, washing dishes, cooking, walking, talking or just sitting quietly. Whatever we do, let us do it as our offering to God.

Words of Wisdom

All work is blessed when we allow God to work
through us to reach others.

—*Proverbs 22:29*

You are never in the wrong place to serve God.
Even if no one acknowledges your efforts, God sees
and knows. Bloom where you are planted.

—*Unknown*

I used to ask God to help me. Then I asked if I
might help Him. I ended up by asking God to
do His work through me.

—*Hudson Taylor*

Lesson 20

Love is the Key

If you wish to know God and understand Him, you must love Him more and more.

The more you love Him, the more you will know Him.

The key to knowledge is—love!

There is a beautiful story by Tolstoy entitled 'He Who Sees His Neighbour Has Seen God'. It tells us of an old and devout shoemaker, who dreams that Jesus Christ is going to visit him the following day. He gets up early next morning, gets the house spick and span, bakes a fresh loaf of bread and prepares some hot soup to serve God when he comes visiting. His preparations for the Divine Guest complete, he sits at the window of his basement dwelling and scans passers-by eagerly, trying to spot Christ among them. Being a shoemaker, and perched as he was at his basement window, he keeps looking at people's shoes and wonders which pair could belong to God.

However, no passer-by comes knocking at his door. He is hungry, but does not feel like eating, lest he should miss God. Just then he sees a woman listlessly walk down the street with a child crying loudly. She looks distraught, and the child is obviously hungry. He invites her to come in, comforts her and gives a bowl of milk for the hungry child. He also offers the mother some soup and bread, and helps her as much as he possibly can.

Back at the window, he sees a man at work, shovelling the accumulated snow, even as he shivers in the bitter winter cold. The shoemaker invites him too to come in and warm himself and share a simple meal with him.

Time passes. Day melts into twilight. The shoemaker waits patiently till midnight. He has not seen Jesus, and disappointed as well as exhausted, he prepares to go to bed. As is his custom, he opens the Bible to read a passage from it before retiring for the night, and finds these words: 'Whatever you did unto one of these, the least of my brethren, you did it unto Me.'

The old shoemaker's heart lifts with joy and love, for he realises that Christ did visit him, not once, but several times in the day in the garb of his needy brothers and sisters.

Understanding

How may we know God? How may we draw closer to God?

All we need to do is let go of the lower self—the ego with its passion and pride—and let God in. For He is our true self, and we are a part of His divine aspect.

When the mind is still, we find God in everything, and we find everything in God! We need nothing, we desire nothing. All we want is to obey His Will.

The one thing we need to do is to focus the mind on God, to live in constant awareness of His presence and dedicate our lives to Him! For God is the goal of our lives and He is to be realised, not merely discussed, defined, understood or explained.

Warming Up

Today, turn to God as often as you can. Think of Him during your daily routine. Pray to Him ever so often, 'I love You God! I want to love You more and more! I want to love You more than anything else in the world. I want to love You to distraction, to intoxication. Grant me pure love and devotion for Thy Lotus Feet, and so bless me that this world-bewitching maya may not lead me astray. And make me, Blessed Master, an instrument of Thy help and healing in this world of suffering and pain.'

The secret of a new life, is given in a few words:

Love God with all thy heart and mind and soul and love thy neighbour as thyself.

Words of Wisdom

But by devotion to Me alone I may thus be perceived, Arjuna, and known and seen in essence and entered, O Parantapa.

—*Gita: XI-54*

God's beneficence streams out from the morning sun, and His love looks down upon us from the starry eyes of midnight. It is His solicitude that wraps us in the air, and the pressure of His Hand, so to speak, that keeps our pulses beating. O! it is a great thing to realise that the Divine Power is always working; that nature, in every valve and every artery, is full of the presence of God.

—*EH Chapin*

Lesson 21

Purpose of Life

The purpose of the human birth is to realise that we all are immortal spirits—not the bodies we wear!

Sri Ramakrishna Paramahansa was about to leave his body and enter into the unseen. He had been suffering from cancer of the throat, and in his last days it became impossible for him to even sip some water. Swami Vivekananda begged the master to pray to Mother Kali that he may at least be able to drink a little water, if not for himself, at least to lessen the anguish and misery of his disciples, who could not bear to see their master in such agony. The master only laughed and replied that his disciples must now eat and drink a little more than usual, because he could only swallow through their throats now! 'I have eaten with my throat for so many years,' he said, 'and God is asking me, "Can you not eat through their throats now?" Why should I depend on this body? This body is rotten and almost gone!'

In those last hours before the master passed away, Sharada Ma became very upset and anxious. Sri Ramakrishna asked her, 'Why do you cry? Because the one who *is*, is not going to die. And did you love this body known as me or did you love the one who *is*?' Sharada Ma answered, with tears, 'I loved the one who *is*.' Sri Ramakrishna replied, 'Then you must stop worrying and crying.'

Sri Ramakrishna passed away on the night of 15 August 1883, at the age of fifty. When Sharada Ma was about to break her bangles, like all Bengali widows, she heard her husband's voice call out to her, 'Sharada, what are you doing? I have not died! I have but passed from one room to another.'

Once we asked Gurudev Sadhu Vaswani to tell us what death really meant. He said, 'Death is a bridge between this world and the next. The next would be a better, nobler, happier, more beautiful, more radiant world than this one.'

He added, 'Death is like sunset, which is only an appearance. When the sun sets here, it is sunrise elsewhere. In reality, the sun never sets. Likewise there is no death. Death is only an appearance, an illusion. For death here, is birth elsewhere.'

Understanding

Everyone fears death. It is difficult to overcome this fear. But the best way to face it perhaps is to sing or recite the Name Divine, constantly. As you sing the Name Divine, keep wishing, and believing, 'The sea is vast; my boat is small. But Thy Name, I know, will take me across!'

When you chant the Name in love and complete faith, all fear of death will vanish from your heart as mist does before the morning sun. You will learn to look upon death as no more than a bridge between you and the Beloved. And you will actually begin to long for the day when you may be called upon to cross this bridge, behold the beauteous Face of the Beloved and abide in His presence for ever and ever more!

Warming Up

Practise this exercise in consciousness at least once a week:

1. Know—that transient are all earthly things and forms. All that you see around will, one day, perish. Everything carries within it the seed of decay. The potter makes earthern vessels; they all must break, one day. Such is the life of man. A man may live a hundred years or longer, yet, he must one day depart. The rich and the poor, the young and the old, the wise and the unwise are all subject to death.

2. This, too, you must know! That there is no escaping death. When the hour arrives, not all the armies of kings and conquerors can save you from death. So it is that while friends and relatives helplessly look on and shed tears, their dearly loved ones are snatched away by death—like animals led to the slaughterhouse.

3. Knowing this, the wise do not grieve over the dead. Grief and lamentation do not bring the dead to life. Rather they add to our suffering and rob us of our richest treasure—peace of mind. The wise ones aspire to peace. They grieve not, nor do they lament. They walk the way of acceptance. They accept whatever comes, and so overcome suffering and sorrow. And having overpowered sorrow they are freed

from it, and can seek the peace that defies description. They are the truly blessed ones.

At the end of this awareness exercise, repeat to yourself, this first commandment of the Gita, 'I am not this body that I wear. I am the immortal soul, the Atman! Weapons cannot cleave me and fire cannot burn me and water cannot wet me and the winds cannot dry me away.'

Words of Wisdom

As a human being puts on new garments, giving
up old ones, the soul similarly accepts new
material bodies, giving up the old and useless ones.

—*Srimad Bhagavad Gita*

The soul can never be cut to pieces by any
weapon, nor burned by fire, nor moistened by
water, nor withered by the wind.

—*Srimad Bhagavad Gita*

If the sight of the blue skies fills you with joy,
if a blade of grass springing up in the fields
has power to move you, if the simple things in
nature have a message you understand, rejoice,
for your soul is alive.

—*Eleanora Duse*

Lesson 22

THE HIDDEN SHAKTI

An infinite potential lies hidden within us. We are unaware of it because we think of ourselves as limited, restricted creatures. We have identified ourselves with the bodies we wear, the biochemical mental organism.

Our true self is the Atman.

Tat twam asi! *That art thou!*

There can be no limit to what we can do and achieve!

The *Chandogya Upanishad* tells us the story of Svetaketu and his father, Uddalaka.

At the right age, Svetaketu was given the sacred thread. Following the *upanayanam,* his father said to him, 'It is time for you now, to proceed to the *gurukul,* so that you may learn the Vedas for there is no one in our family who is not learned in the sacred scriptures.'

As directed by his father, Svetaketu went to a *gurukul*—the ashram of a guru and studied the Vedas under the guru. He returned home when he was twenty-four years of age, a proud scholar. He thought that there was very little that he did not know.

His father was a wise and perceptive man. From the very gait, demeanour and appearance of his son, he realised that his scholarship had only turned Svetaketu arrogant and egoistic.

'Son, I think you feel you have mastered all knowledge on the face of the earth,' he said. 'But pray tell me, have you ever learnt that knowledge by which you can hear what is not heard, perceive what cannot be perceived and know what cannot be known?'

Svetaketu was both perplexed and upset. 'How can such instruction be imparted?' he asked his father humbly. 'Father, won't you tell me what that knowledge is?'

Judging the time to be ripe, his father began, 'My dear, let me explain myself fully. When, for instance, you know one clod of clay, you can know all that is made of clay. When you know a nugget of gold, you can know all ornaments made of gold, because the essence of it is gold. The only difference is in their names and forms. That is the knowledge I am talking about.'

Svetaketu said, 'Father, my venerable gurus did not perhaps know it. Had they known, why would they have not taught it to me? So please, you teach it to me.'

Uddalaka agreed, 'Alright. I shall teach you. Listen. In the beginning of creation, O Child, the *Sat* or True Being alone existed. It had neither equal nor second. It thought, Let me multiply myself and create beings. He first created *Tejas* or fire god. The fire god wanted to multiply himself. He created the water god. The water god wanted to multiply himself and created the food god. Then the True Being thought, I have now created these three gods. Now I shall enter them as *Jiva-atman*, and assume name and form!

'He or the *Sat* alone is all-name, because every name is His Name. He alone is all-power because every power is His. All the forms that belong to others are reflections of His form. He is the only one without an equal or second. He is the best of all. He being the Chief, He is called *Sat* or the True Being. Knowing Him, we know everything else. When a man sleeps soundly, he comes into contact with the *Sat*. When man dies, his speech merges in the mind, the mind in his breath, his breath in the fire and the fire in the Highest God, the True Being. Thus, the soul or *Jiva-atman* is deathless. All the universe is controlled by the *Sat*. He pervades it all. He is the destroyer of all. He is full of perfect qualities.

'My child, the rivers that run in the different directions rise from the sea and go back to the sea. Yet, the sea remains the same. The rivers, while in the sea, cannot identify themselves as one particular river or another. So also creatures that have come from *Sat* know not that they have come from that *Sat*, although they become one or the other again and again.'

Uddalaka then asked his son to bring a fig fruit. When he did so, Uddalaka asked him to break it. He broke it.

'What do you see in it?' asked Uddalaka.

Svetaketu replied, 'I see small seeds.'

'Break one of the seeds and tell me what you see.'

'Nothing, father.'

'You are unable to see the minute particles of the seed, yet the mighty tree is born out of that essence of that particle. Like that, the True Being is the essence of all creation.'

Uddalaka then asked his son to bring some salt and put it into a bowl of water.

Svetaketu did so. His father asked him to take the salt out.

'I am unable to find the salt, father,' said Svetaketu, 'for it has dissolved.'

Uddalaka then asked his son to taste some of the water. It was obviously salty, and Svetaketu said so.

Uddalaka said to him, 'Now child, you do not see the salt, although you know it is certainly in the water. Thus, the True Being is the subtle essence present everywhere in this universe, although you do not see Him. He is the essence of all, and the desired of all. He is known to the subtlest intellect. That is the self. That is the truth. That art thou, Svetaketu. *Tat twam asi.*'

UNDERSTANDING

The world of nature, all the aspects of the wide and vast universe that God has created, is full of the most potent energy and the most positive vibrations. If ever you are feeling 'low' or mentally exhausted, go outdoors to breathe in the fresh air. Take it in, and as you inhale, tell yourself, 'I am connecting to the universe God has made. Let its positive energy flow into me.'

This simple activity will make a great difference to your well-being and attitude!

Warming Up

Today, repeat to yourself as often as you can, whenever you can find the time, 'I am not this body that I wear. I am the immortal Spirit, the Atman!'

Words of Wisdom

He who knows self as the enjoyer of the honey from the flowers of the senses, ever present within, ruler of time, goes beyond fear. For this self is supreme!

—*The Upanishads*

The power of God is with you at all times through the activities of mind, senses, breathing and emotions, and is constantly doing all the work using you as a mere instrument.

—*Srimad Bhagavad Gita*

Men often become what they believe themselves to be. If I believe I cannot do something, it makes me incapable of doing it. But when I believe I can, then I acquire the ability to do it even if I didn't have it in the beginning.

—*Mahatma Gandhi*

Lesson 23

Words of Power

When all around us the storms blow and the tempests roar, let us close our eyes, think of God and repeat the words, 'God is with me, and He is in control.'

These are powerful words that can quell the fiercest storm.

The famous Scottish preacher, John McNeil, once related this moving personal incident from his life:

As a boy, little John went to work at a place far away from home. Everyday he had to walk back home through a dense forest and across a lonely ravine. People said wild animals and notorious criminals roamed the ravine. Little John would dread to cross the ravine, wondering everyday, what if…what if…?

One night, he got back from work very late. The moon had hid behind dark, threatening clouds. The ravine thus loomed ahead in pitch darkness. The little boy made his way gingerly across, his heart numb with cold terror. And then, he heard footfalls of someone behind him, a voice too called out from a distance.

John McNeil stopped. He couldn't take another step. He held onto his breath, too terrified to even exhale! He could hear the person closing in; the voice called out to him clearly then, 'John, John!'

It was his father's voice!

Knowing that the boy was late and aware of his deep fear of the ravine, John's father had come out to greet his son and cross the ravine with him that night.

Out of the darkness, the loving father figure emerged and took the boy by the hand. The boy felt the father's arms around him, and it was the sweetest and most wonderful sensation of his life!

'His coming changed the whole experience for me,' John McNeil would recall, in later days.

God is your Father and my Father. In times of despair and darkness, we can hear His voice for He will unfailingly come to meet us. He will be there when we need Him. All we have to do is trust Him absolutely and completely.

Understanding

There was a disciple, who asked his master to help him develop the right attitude to life and work.

'How can I acquire discipline in my search for truth?'

'You must exercise yourself,' replied the master.

'How may I exercise myself?'

'You must eat when you are hungry; you must sleep when you are tired.'

'But...,' stammered the disciple. 'That's what everyone does.'

'But that is exactly what most people do *not* do!' the master asserted. 'When they eat, they are worrying about one hundred things. When they sleep, they dream of one thousand things. This is not the kind of exercise I meant!'

The Zen master in fact, had uttered a great truth! Most of us are unable to engage ourselves fully even in the routine tasks of everyday life. The reason? We do not live in the present. We are drowning in the regrets and disappointments of the past. Or losing our balance in vague imaginative anxieties about the future. What we fail to realise is that life would be so much more satisfying and meaningful, and we ourselves will be happier and more peaceful, if we learn to live in the present—walking with God today and trusting Him for the morrow!

When you feel that He is taking care of your needs, you cease to worry! You do not have to plan in advance for unforeseen eventualities. You do not have to worry about calamities. You simply allow the Divine Plan to unfold. You claim nothing; you ask nothing; you seek nothing; you plan nothing. You simply become a channel for the Divine Plan to flow through.

How many of us are capable of such faith and trust?

Warming Up

Let your mantra for today be, 'God is in control!'

In God's Providence, everything comes to pass at the right time.

The sun rises at the right time; the stars appear at the right time; the seasons change at the right time.

Put forth the best that you are capable of. Leave the results in the safe Hands of the Lord. He will never fail you!

Leave it to God, and He will take care of everything!

Words of Wisdom

Frequently remind yourself that God is with
you, that He will never fail you, that you can
count upon Him.
Say these words, 'God is with me, helping me.'

—*Norman Vincent Peale*

Open your hearts to the love God instills...
God loves you tenderly.
What He gives you is not to be kept under lock
and key, but to be shared.

—*Mother Teresa*

Lesson 24

ENLIGHTENMENT!

No man can attain enlightenment riding only on his own efforts. Enlightenment cometh to man by the Grace of God. Do strive for enlightenment. But be like the peasant who tills the soil and sows the seed, and then turns to the heavens for chandi ka gola*—the silver drops of rain.*

Milarepa was a great Tibetan yogi, whose name has spread around the globe. There is a touching incident related to him. One day, Milarepa approached a guru and begged to be accepted as a disciple. Guru Marpa then asked him, 'Do you have sufficient faith?'

Milarepa answered with humility, 'Master, my faith in you is beyond words.'

But the guru wanted to test him first. 'Here are some bricks,' he told Milarepa. 'Build a platform at this spot.'

Milarepa immediately set to work. He worked hard and built a platform that looked good and was also sturdy. He was confident that it would please his guru. But when the guru saw it, he exclaimed, 'What a fool you are, Milarepa! You have wasted your time and energy. I did not want a platform here, at this corner, but there, at that corner!'

After, few more days of hard labour, the second platform was ready. Once again, the guru was dissatisfied. 'You are an idiot! I did not want the platform here!'

Milarepa controlled his irritation and disappointment. He built a third platform. It too met the same fate, the guru rejected it outright.

The act was repeated again and again. Finally, Milarepa reached the end of his patience. His self-control was dwindling. And faith was completely shaken. He now only wanted to run away from the guru, never to return.

The guru's wife learned of his frustration. She came to his rescue. 'The guru is only testing you!' she revealed. 'It was you who told him that your faith in him was beyond words—limitless as the sky. Where has this faith gone?'

Her words had a profound effect. Milarepa's faith was renewed. He built yet another platform. When it was ready, the guru embraced him, saying, 'You are truly my child. Let me share with you the secret I have shared with none else!'

Milarepa then sat at the feet of the guru and received from him what only a guru could pass on to his disciple. He was enlightened. He was liberated from the seemingly endless cycle of birth, death and rebirth.

The guru, like God, is too loving to punish and too wise to make a mistake. Therefore, let us learn to accept his will. For in his will is our salvation and our enlightenment.

Understanding

A great guru outlined the following as the vital aspects of guru-bhakti:

1) Absolute faith in the thoughts, words and actions of the guru.

2) Perfect obedience in carrying out the guru's commands.

3) Offering devoted service to the guru without expectation of reward.

4) Self-surrender or dedication of all that we are and all that we have—*tan, man, dhan*—body, mind and wealth, at the lotus feet of the guru.

5) The guru knows better than I do, and he is always right! I am always wrong.

6) Look out for opportunities to be of service to the guru. When such an opportunity occurs, grab it. Do not be complacent.

Why is guru-bhakti so essential today?

Guru-bhakti yoga is something that all of us can practise in this *kaliyuga*. It is the shortest, easiest and quickest way to reach God. The practice of this yoga frees us from our ego and enables us to cross this difficult worldly ocean—*sansar sagar*. Obeying the will of the guru is a great virtue, for it negates self-will, ego and indiscipline, and inculcates the divine qualities of humility, self-surrender and devotion.

Alas, obedience is becoming conspicuous by its fast disappearance in the world today! The values we worship are aggression, self-assertion, the ability to have one's own way, the strength to impose our will on others, the power to get everybody to do what we want them to do!

The questioning spirit is good in certain matters, but we must not question basic values.

Obedience has but one meaning—to obey. I may deliver a hundred discourses on obedience and write multiple volumes on the subject. but I have not advanced a single step if I have not learnt to obey. The way of obedience leads to the way of surrender, of which the Gita speaks in such rapturous terms.

One essential mark of the true disciple is implicit obedience of the guru's wishes. 'Not my will, but the guru's will be done,' says the true disciple at every step. And the more he is attuned to the guru's will, the more he will grow in the likeness of the guru, until one blessed day, the disciple becomes a part of the guru's being. The disciple flows into the guru; the guru flows into the disciple. The twain are one, one in the One who is peace, joy and bliss!

WARMING UP

Today, learn to overcome needless anxiety. Do not be overanxious about anything, even about your spiritual progress. For remember, He who is our Lord and Master, the *Satguru* knows what is best for us, and if He wishes us to go slow, He knows best; there must be wisdom in it. Therefore, do not fret.

To be unduly concerned is to waste a lot of energy, which may otherwise be used for a good purpose. Learn to resign yourself in His Will. 'Thy Will be done!' Let this be the one prayer of your heart. 'Not mine, but Thy will be done, O Lord!'

Words of Wisdom

Through selfless work, love of God grows in the heart. Then, through His Grace one may realise Him in course of time. God can be seen. One can talk to Him as I am talking to you.

—*Sri Ramakrishna*

Few souls understand what God would accomplish in them if they were to abandon themselves unreservedly to Him and if they were to allow His Grace to mould them accordingly.

—*St Ignatius of Loyola*

Lesson 25

THERE IS NO DEATH

The greatest illusion from which man suffers is perhaps the illusion of death. In reality, there is no death. Death is very much like the sunset. When the sun sets here, it has already risen elsewhere. Likewise, death here is birth elsewhere. For life is eternal.

I read about a yogi many years ago. He was the only son of a rich businessman. His father, a rich merchant, suddenly passed away and the son said to himself, 'My father has moved on, leaving all the wealth behind; this wealth was of no use to him. He could not carry one single paisa along with him. Of what use will all this wealth be to me?' And so he distributes all his wealth to the poor and retires to the solitude of the Himalayan heights. There he goes and lives a life of meditation. As days pass, he meditates more and more. He sinks deeper and deeper into himself, until one blessed day, in the lotus of the heart within, he beholds the shining Face of God. He meets God face to face. And then, as he opens his eyes, he finds the one Face of God, the one Divine Face in everything, in everyone around him. God in the mountains, God in the stone, God in the tree, God in the shrub, God in the plant, God in the animal, God in every man, God in every grain of sand, God in every drop of water, God in every ray of sunshine. And he begins to exclaim:

Jidhar dekhta hoon, udhar Tu hi Tu hai!
Ke har shai mein jalwa Tera hubahu hai!

Wherever I turn, I behold Thee Lord!
In everything I see, I perceive Thy splendour.

This is the experience of every true yogi.

And then he descends from the mountain heights. To the plains below.

He treks down to the villages, where the poor and broken dwell. And carries with him many medicinal herbs. Moving from one cottage to another, he distributes these herbs to the sick and needy. He approaches them with love. And speaks to them. He looks closely into their needs. And shows them the way to true happiness—ananda. But everyday, in the morning and in the evening, he sits under a tree and meditates.

One day, while he is sitting under a tree in meditation, the king of Benaras, arrogant of his stately power, and intoxicated with drink, happens to pass by. His glance falls on the yogi. The king walks up to him and asks, 'O, you who sit with closed eyes, tell me what is it that you teach?'

The yogi does not respond, not even opening his eyes. The king feels offended. He unsheathes his sword and waving it before the yogi, threatens, 'If you will not open your eyes, if you will not give me an answer, I shall kill you.'

The yogi then opens his eyes. And looking quietly, gently and lovingly into the face of the king replies, 'O King, you cannot kill me for I am deathless. I am immortal. I am immutable. I am eternal. You can only destroy this body.'

The king is amazed at the fearlessness of this yogi. And he feels ashamed of his conduct. He looks into the eyes of the yogi and finds them aglow with a strange, mystic light. Struck with awe, the king falls down at the feet of the yogi and begs for forgiveness. And he says to the yogi, 'O Yogi, do kindly tell me, what is it that you teach?' The yogi then replies, 'O King, this is what I teach. Cleanse your heart. Be humble. And give the service of love to all who suffer and are in pain.'

In these few and simple words, we find the very essence of what yoga stands for. These words resonate the very secret of the life of a yogi.

UNDERSTANDING

Do not be a miser; do not cling to the body, you must spend your infinite spiritual wealth. Free yourself of ignorance; let go of the ego; rid yourself of the humiliating notion that you are limited by your body and mind. Realise that you belong to infinity, that your soul is immortal, that God's power and Grace sustain you and that you are essentially divine!

Warming Up

Today practise the sadhana of focusing on your breathing. Follow your breath with the mind. When the mind is fixed on the inhaled and exhaled breath, it gets trained to be part of the universal breath of life, and in time, realises that its true dwelling place is not this body.

Words of Wisdom

As person abandons worn-out clothes and
acquires new ones, so when the body is worn-
out, a new one is acquired by the self,
who lives within.

—*Srimad Bhagavad Gita*

For the soul, there is neither birth nor death,
at anytime. He has not come into being, does
not come into being and will not come into
being. He is unborn, eternal, ever-existing and
primeval. He is not slain when the body is slain.

—*Srimad Bhagavad Gita*

Lesson 26

Free from Anger and Arrogance

The greatest intoxication is that of the ego. The worst madness is that of anger.

The person who is free from arrogance and anger, finds goodness and beauty wherever he goes.

Let me tell you the story of Shuka Muni, son of the great Rishi Ved Vyasa. Shuka was born a *jnani*. It is said that when he was only in his mother's womb, he decided not to take birth on this earth, which was surrounded by maya. But Rishi Vyasa wanted a son desperately. The Lord thus suspended maya temporarily so that Shuka could take birth. Such was this *jnani*, who went on to become a great yogi, blessed with astounding powers and deep knowledge.

One day, Shuka had this desire to ascend to Vaikunth and behold Sri Vishnu. His yogic powers took him to the doors of the Lord's abode immediately. But here, he was stopped from entering inside. The reason? One who had not sat at the feet of the guru could not gain entry to the Lord's abode.

Bitterly disappointed, Shuka returned to Rishi Ved Vyasa and begged him to provide guru *bodhana*—teaching. Although Sage Vyasa was a great guru, he in his wisdom knew that he could not help his son in this predicament. So he advised Shuka, 'Seek initiation at the feet of King Janaka for he is an enlightened being. He is the one who can illumine your soul.'

Shuka was flabbergasted. How could a king, living in the lap of luxury, and ruling the country with all the worldliness it entailed, offer him initiation? With great reluctance, he went to King Janaka's palace. To his horror, he found the king seated on a golden throne, studded with diamonds. Beautiful maids were fanning him and pressing his hands and feet. Seven hundred queens surrounded him.

Shuka was repulsed by the sight. He himself was a great ascetic. What could the sensual king teach him? He returned from the palace disgusted.

'Did you see the king?' his father enquired upon his return. 'I did,' replied Shuka. 'But I don't think he is going to be of any use to me. He is a worldly man, trapped in his worldly wealth. How can such a one enlighten *me*?'

'You are mistaken,' Sage Vyasa countered. 'Do not be taken in by appearances. There is no greater preceptor than Janaka whom I can recommend to you.'

Shuka went back to Janaka's court, but returned empty-handed again, shocked by the royal splendour he saw everywhere.

'What happened?' asked his father. 'Did you receive what you wanted from the king?'

'There is *nothing* I can receive from him,' was the disgruntled response.

'Dear son, go back to him and try again,' insisted Vyasa.

Again Shuka went to Janaka's court, and returned without the enlightenment he sought. This happened twelve times.

On the thirteenth trip, he encountered an old man, who was throwing fistfuls of mud into the fast-flowing river. The mud dissolved and disappeared without a trace in the flooded river, yet the old man kept on at his task.

'Foolish old man,' cried Shuka, 'what do you hope to achieve with this futile effort?'

'Foolish? I'm not half as foolish as Shuka, son of the great Sage Ved Vyasa, who could not recognise truth when he saw it. He is the real fool, for he knows not that it is only Janaka who can give him the knowledge he seeks!'

Stunned, Shuka fell at the old man's feet. The old man revealed himself to be none other than Maharishi Narada, who had come down to offer the young man guidance. 'Go back to Janaka,' he said to Shuka. 'Your father is right; Janaka is the one to offer you enlightenment.'

Chastened and subdued, Shuka returned to Janaka's palace. For the first time, in his thirteenth visit, he was stopped at the gate by guards who enquired the purpose of his visit. When he told them what he wanted, they took his message to the king. Janaka instructed them to keep him waiting outside the palace for three whole days.

For three days, Shuka stood outside the palace gates. On the third day, he was led inside to the inner apartments where the royal ladies lived. Here, he was surrounded by every sensual pleasure that a human being could imagine. The great ascetic that he was, Shuka was unmoved, unaffected by it all. Thus, three more days passed.

Finally, the king sent for him. When Shuka entered the king's presence, he was stunned by the sight that met his eyes. The king was seated on his magnificent throne; his right leg was being luxuriously massaged with perfumed oil and sandal paste, while his left leg was placed in a blazing fire!

Progressively, Shuka's ego had been diminishing. His perception had been clouded by his pride in the self, and he had failed to see what Janaka really was. Now, he saw that Janaka was much more than the wealthy, sensual king he had beheld from the outside; he was truly an evolved soul, blessed with realisation and not trapped by renunciation or materialism, undefined by sensuality or extreme self-denial.

Shuka prostrated before the king and begged for enlightenment.

'Now, you are indeed ready to become my disciple,' Janaka proclaimed. 'You have realised that perception can be clouded by ego, and that pride is useless and, above all, that only consciousness is real.'

Janaka touched Shuka and gave him a mantra, and instantly, Shuka felt himself transformed. He had discovered the self within. It had always been within him, but he had been unconscious of it due to his rampant ego. When a man loses his ego, he discovers God within him!

Understanding

The true guru can destroy your false ego and lead you on to the God within you.

The guru spells death to the ego. He does not have to implant God within you, because He already exists there. All the guru does is clean away the accumulated dirt that has soiled the mirror of your heart, and when the ugly stains of the ego are removed, you behold the Beloved reflected therein.

There are many modern Shuka munis among us even today. They go forth from one guru to another, rejecting each for one reason or another. They are haunted by their own ego, their pride of knowledge and arrogance over their sadhana. They imagine they are perfectly apt in meditation and renunciation, and need the guru only for the sake of name. The guru must then perform 'surgery' on their ego, before they can receive anything from him.

'I know this…I can do this…I am such a one…I am the doer…I am the giver.' How vain and futile are such assertions! Here is how a great poet saint puts it:

When my ego was struck by the sword that is the guru's love,
That love began to kill my ego.
Even when I was alive, I experienced death.
My death died; I became immortal.

Warming Up

How may the ego be annihilated?

1) When in the midst of friends or strangers, refrain from pushing yourself forward. Watch how at the slightest excuse, there arises the tendency to show yourself off.

2) Refrain from too much talk. The less you talk, the less you will be noticed and the more you will be permitted to recede into the background.

As it is, we tend to talk too much. Some of us constantly try to monopolise the conversation. Sometimes, friends come to us to unburden themselves, and instead of listening to them with understanding and sympathy, we overwhelm them with our discourse on endurance and patience. Oh how we love 'lecturing' others! If only we could remain silent and let others talk, it would do us a world of good.

3) Always check the desire to tell others about your life and achievements, your inner struggles and experiences, your opinions and aspirations. Learn to live and grow in the thought that you are a tiny particle of dust, and that no one will miss you when you are away.

4) Remember, your real value lies not in your outer, empirical self, but in your inner, imperishable self, and this inner self cares not for the applause of others. It is firmly established in itself.

5) Cultivate friendship with this inner self. And meditate on the significant words of the Gita:

> He who hath conquered
> His lower self of cravings and desires,
> He hath his Supreme Friend found
> In the self, immortal, true!
>
> But he who still a victim is
> To his appetites and passions,
> Verily, the self becometh to him,
> Hostile as an enemy!

Words of Wisdom

All troubles come to an end when the ego dies.

—Sri Ramakrishna

It is on account of the ego that one is not able to see God. In front of the door of God's mansion lies the stump of ego. One cannot enter the mansion without jumping over the stump.

—Sri Ramakrishna

The ego's phenomenal existence is transcended when you dive into the source from where the 'I'-thought rises.

—Ramana Maharshi

Remove the ego and *avidya*—ignorance is gone.
Look for it, the ego vanishes and the real self
alone remains.

—*Ramana Maharshi*

Ego has a voracious appetite. The more you feed it,
the hungrier it gets.

—*Nathaniel Bronner Jr*

Lesson 27

Insults are Like Bad Coins

Has someone offended or insulted you?

Insults are like bad coins. You cannot avoid them, but you can always refuse to accept them.

Purna was one of Buddha's devoted disciples. He wished to spread his master's message among the people of Sronapranta. Now, it was well-known that the people of Sronapranta were wild and ferocious. No preacher's life was safe in their country. Purna's plan thus appeared preposterous to many of his fellow *bhikkus,* who began to fear for his life.

But Purna was a man of faith. There was no fear in his heart for it was filled through and through with love for all living creatures, and profound compassion for those who live in the darkness of ignorance.

So he went to seek Buddha's blessings. The master said to him, 'Purna, you know very well that the people of Sronapranta are wild and ferocious. They insult and slander one another, and are prone to fits of anger, such that they lose all control. Now, if they insult and abuse you, and vent their wrath on you, what will you do?'

'If at all they abuse and insult me, Master,' said Purna, 'I shall still think them to be kind and friendly, for they have not beaten or stoned me.'

'And what if they beat you or stone you?'

'I would still regard them as being kind as they have not attacked me with weapons.'

'And if,' asked Buddha, 'they should attack you with weapons...?'

'Then, too,' answered Purna, 'I would regard them as kind and friendly as they have not killed me.'

'And what if they kill you, Purna?'

'Even if they kill me, Master,' said Purna, 'I shall thank them at the moment of my death for they will be liberating me from the limitations of the body and the bonds of human life!'

The Blessed One was very pleased with Purna's answers. 'You are gifted with the greatest gentleness and patience,' he said. 'You may go and dwell among the people of Sronapranta. Show them the way to be free, even as you are free!'

Blessed was Purna! He was free; he was fearless. He then showed the people of Sronapranta how they could be free and fearless too. Running after pleasures, accumulating more and more possessions or acquiring much earthly power was not the right approach. You must not adopt the way of *preya*—the smooth and slippery way of ease and comfort. But go the way of *shreya*—the tough and difficult path. *Shreya* is the path that ushers in you the awareness that you are very near and dear to God.

UNDERSTANDING

There are so many bitter experiences, so many incidents that trouble us, and we are unable to understand the *why* of them. We must learn to look upon all these experiences—pleasant and unpleasant, as opportunities to learn more about ourselves and our lives. Experiences are not harsh or bitter in themselves; they come to teach valuable lessons that are necessary for us to evolve. We should thus accept every experience as *prasadam* handed out by God.

People often exclaim, 'I feel like tearing my hair!' or 'I feel like banging my head against a wall!' This happens when they get very irritated or frustrated. But when his daughters' behaviour began to get on his frayed nerves, what did King Lear say? He exclaimed, 'Let me not be mad, not mad, sweet Heaven!'

If we tear our hair, shed bitter tears or bang our heads against a wall, we would only add to our problems. This is a very negative reaction and will not solve our problems at all. What is happening will surely happen; we cannot avoid it; we cannot escape it, we cannot alter it. But we do have a choice: To react to it in a negative way, or respond to it in a positive way. The latter will save much of your precious emotional energy.

Warming Up

Today, be on the lookout for a person—friend or colleague or acquaintance, who insults you or vexes you, knowingly or unknowingly. When it happens, you will undoubtedly be very quick to react in kind! But since you are practising this awareness technique, pause before you react instinctively, and then respond in a more mature way to the insult. Control your anger; resist the impulse to trade more insults; swallow self-pity; smile at the person and then watch his or her reaction.

Words of Wisdom

When an evil man, seeing you practise goodness, comes and maliciously insults you, you should patiently endure it and not feel angry with him, for the evil man is insulting himself by trying to insult you.

—*Gautama Buddha*

A wise man is superior to any insults, which can be put upon him, and the best reply to unseemly behaviour is patience and moderation.

—*Moliere*

Lesson 28

The Test of a Man

The test of a man is—how much he can bear and how much he can share, and how soon he confesses a mistake and makes amends for it.

According to Kabir's teachings, the first principle of righteous living is to revere the guest, to welcome and serve him as though he were an image of God. A guest is called an *atithi*, which means one who announces himself without previous intimation. This, said Kabir, is a quality of God, so the guest must be treated as God.

Sant Kabir himself practised this ideal and lovingly served guests and sadhus who came to his hut unannounced. His hut was a small one and could contain only four beds. Almost everyday there were some guests to be looked after. And the four beds were occupied by the guests. The members of the family would gladly sleep on the floor. The food would first be served to the guests, and what was left over would be eaten by the family members. Yet, all the four regarded themselves as among the happiest of humans.

We are told that one evening, when it was raining very heavily, a few sadhus arrived at the cottage of Sant Kabir and said to him, 'We have heard a lot about you and your spirit of hospitality. Can we be your guests for a few hours and share a meal with you?'

Sant Kabir welcomed them with open arms and a warm heart. He asked his wife, Loi, what food she could serve to the guests. Loi replied that right then there was nothing in the house which could be offered to the guests; all the groceries had been consumed.

Kabir told his wife that he had woven some cloth, and they could sell it. But, unfortunately, the bazaar was closed, and besides, it was raining heavily. When the rain stopped, he would go and sell the cloth. In the meantime, he asked her if there was any shop nearby from where they could get some groceries on credit.

Loi replied, 'Beloved, you know very well, there is no shop that would give us food on credit. As we are poor, they always ask for money first, and only then give us groceries.'

Kabir was unperturbed. He said, 'God who has sent those guests will Himself provide food for them.'

He asked his wife to go to the market and try her luck. Some shopkeeper might agree to give her the required groceries on credit. Loi obediently went from one shop to another, asking for credit. But no one was prepared to oblige. At last, she reached a shop whose owner was a young man. Loi was a pretty woman. The young man looked at her and said, he would oblige on the condition that she spend the night with him.

Loi was appalled to hear this. How could any man utter such words to a married woman? Thinking that she had agreed to his condition, the shopkeeper told her to take whatever she needed. Loi brought the commodities home and served the guests. They were gratified to be served so well.

When the guests had departed, Loi narrated the story of the young shopkeeper to her husband. Sant Kabir said to his wife, 'It is getting dark and the young man must be waiting for you. I shall take you there, but as it is still raining heavily, cover yourself with a blanket.'

Sant Kabir carried his wife, Loi on his shoulders and arrived at the house of the shopkeeper. He waited outside the house while Loi went in. The shop owner was astonished to see her. Despite the heavy downpour, he found that her clothes were dry and her feet were clean. Loi explained to him that it was her husband who had brought her on his own shoulders. Hearing this, the shop owner was taken aback.

How could a husband bring his own wife in the dark of the night to the house of a man whose intentions were impure!

The shopkeeper realised that the husband was no ordinary man, and he felt extremely guilty. He felt ashamed of his conduct. He wanted to know more about her husband.

Loi revealed to the young man, 'His name is Sant Kabir, and he is waiting outside.'

The shop owner, with tears in his eyes, asked Loi to forgive him for his misconduct. He fell at the feet of Sant Kabir and begged for mercy. Kabir embraced him and said that he had been forgiven and must now forget all that had happened. From then on, the shopkeeper became a faithful disciple of Sant Kabir, and said to him, 'Henceforth, my shop and all it contains belong to you!'

Understanding

The causes of human restlessness are not far to seek:

- Constant seeking of objects flares into passion—*kama.*
- When passion is thwarted, it inflames the anger—*krodha.*
- Anger leads to loss of reason and sanity, and we pass into a state of delusion—*sammoha.*
- In this state of delusion, we lose our memory—*smriti*. We lose the memory of our guru's *upadesh*, the memory of our life's great ideals.
- Losing this memory, we also lose the power of discrimination; we lose reason—*buddhi.*

Let me sum up, in the words of Sadhu Vaswani:

> When the mind is bewildered, confused, you forget the lesson of experience; that is loss of memory. Forgetting experience, you lose discrimination. Losing discrimination, you miss the purpose of life. It is the real loss of man himself.

So the question is: How can we stop ourselves from losing our very humanity?

There are so many ignoble tendencies, so many negative emotions that dwell in all of us. Not only must we rule them and check them with reason and will power, but also by the exercise of the spirit, and by the greatness of our soul.

'Love, love, love thine enemies,' Sadhu Vaswani said, 'and though they hate thee as a thorn, thou wilt bloom as a rose.'

The secret of a happy, carefree and stress-free life is: Love life; love your fellow human beings; love this beautiful world you live in and above all, love the Lord. Then you too, will bloom like a rose!

WARMING UP

Take care of your present thought, and you will change the course of your life.

A man who becomes aware of God's presence will never do any evil.

People often ask me, 'The world is full of cruelties, violence, wars and battles, there is no value for human life, there are so many bomb blasts and people die in thousands. What is the reason?'

The reason is that man is not afraid of God. Man does not realise that God is a witness to his misdeeds. If you would imbibe in your life just three things: God is watching me. God is watching over me. God is witnessing me, your life will make a U-turn. Then you will not hurt or harm anyone, even in your thoughts. You will not think evil of others, because God's omnipresence has become real to you.

Carry this message with you today and translate it into deeds of daily living:

> God is watching me,
> God is watching over me,
> God is witnessing me.

Words of Wisdom

Mistakes are always forgivable, if one has the courage to admit them.

—*Bruce Lee*

Show me a person who has never made a mistake, and I'll show you someone who has never achieved much.

—*Joan Collins*

It's okay to make mistakes. Mistakes are our teachers—they help us to learn.

—*John Bradshaw*

The greatest mistake a man can ever make is to be afraid of making one.

—*Elbert Hubbard*

Lesson 29

Why?

If while praying we can think of worldly matters, why can we not while doing worldly things, think of God?

A long time ago, before you and I were born, and when the world was a much better place, there was a simple farmer who lived happily in a small village. This farmer used to work hard for his living, tilling his crops from morn to night. He took a simple pride in his work and was never happier than when he was in his field. The farmer believed devoutly in God and prayed to him three times a day: Once, before starting his work, the second time before having his lunch and the third time before going to bed.

One day, Narada approached Lord Vishnu and asked him, 'Lord, you have so many followers all over the world. But tell me, among all of them, who is your favourite devotee?' Vishnu smiled and replied, 'I love all my devotees, but yes, there is a farmer in a small village whom I love and admire more than the others.'

Hearing this, Narada, became extremely curious, and set out at once to learn why this farmer was Lord Vishnu's favourite. Now, it so happened that this farmer was the same one we were talking about in the beginning of the story. Narada observed the farmer from high up in the heavens for a few weeks, and then returned to Vishnu, very confused. He confronted Vishnu with his questions. 'Lord,' he said 'I have observed the farmer, and I am very disappointed. He only takes your name three times a day, and the rest of his time he devotes to working in his field and taking care of his family. He has done nothing extraordinary. Why then have you singled him out as your favourite devotee, placing him above the many sages who devote their entire lives meditating on your greatness?'

Lord Vishnu smiled and said, 'Narada, the answer to this question lies in a task I am going to set for you. You must carry this bowl filled with oil in your hands and go around Vaikunth.'

Narada started laughing as the task sounded so easy. 'But, let me warn you,' continued Lord Vishnu, 'not a single drop must spill from the bowl, otherwise, you will fail in your quest.' Narada agreed, and carefully holding the bowl, which was filled to the brim with oil, began his journey around the world.

At the outset, Narada was convinced it was a very simple task, but very soon, he learnt how wrong he had been. It required utmost concentration to balance the bowl in his hands so as to ensure not a single drop spilled from it. Carefully and slowly, step by step, Narada finally completed this difficult task and approached Vishnu, tired and worn-out.

However, he was still wondering why the farmer was Lord Vishnu's favourite. Lord Vishnu greeted him warmly and congratulated him on completing the task successfully. He then asked Narada, 'Tell me, Narada, when you were holding the bowl carefully and going around Vaikunth, how many times did you take my name or think of me?'

Narada was taken aback at the question and stammered, 'But Lord...I did not have the time to think of you...I was so busy concentrating on the bowl of oil. How can you expect me to carry out the difficult task you set for me and think of you at the same time? It is impossible!'

Lord Vishnu then answered gravely, 'Narada, the farmer, who is my best devotee carries out a difficult task everyday—he tends his crops and takes care of his family. It is a task that I have assigned to him, which takes up all his time. Yet, he still finds the time to think of me and pray to me, not just once, but three times a day. And you, who take my name everyday, could not find the time to think of me when you were carrying out your task. This is the difference between all the others and the farmer. I love all my children, but I love them all the more when they do their work uncomplainingly, are good to others and think of me at least once during the day. That is all I ask of them.'

Narada then begged forgiveness, and after thanking the Lord, went away, much enlightened.

Understanding

The famous Sufi dervish, Sultan Bhahu tells us in his *bani*:

> Neither am I a yogi, nor have I practised austerities,
>
> No siddhi have I attained.
>
> The moment I have not remembered the Lord,
>
> I am condemned to be an atheist!

There are many 'yogis' who claim to have attained miraculous powers—especially, hatha yogis. Some of them are known to have been buried alive for two weeks; yet others hang upside-down from the branches of a tree for days on end; some swallow poison; a few eat up pieces of glass. All these acts are considered to be a powerful demonstration of the siddhi they have attained.

But Bhahu insists, 'I have not attained any siddhi, any yogic shakti.'

Indeed, the truth of the matter is that we cannot attain God through such practices and tantras. We often believe that such acts can take us to the state of samadhi that we seek. But the true state of samadhi is one in which we behold the Lord, wherever we turn.

Jo dam gaafil so dam kafir

In that instant when you forget the Lord, at that very instant you become a kafir—a *nastik* or a non-believer.

Who is the atheist? Not just he who denies God, but he who forgets God. How many of us regard ourselves as pious souls, believers! But we do not remember God even for an instant, we become atheists for that instant.

Warming Up

It is said that cancer is the most feared killer disease today. Even worse than cancer is forgetfulness, for oblivion of the Lord means oblivion of our true identity. We often forget the Lord, and lose the meaning of existence. Let us try and focus our thoughts constantly upon the Lord. The heart that is focused upon the Lord is ever at peace.

Let us surrender the thread of our existence in God's hands. When we have done this, we can conquer all difficulties and trials that confront us. Let us think of the Lord, even as we go about our daily duties.

In truth, God loves us all—believers and non believers; the wicked and the virtuous; those who sing His praises and those who deny Him. God is always thinking of us. But we can feel His tremendous love, realise His closeness to us, only when *we* think of Him with love and devotion in our hearts.

Therefore, let us think of God constantly. Before we begin each task, let us pray, 'O Lord, without Your help, without Your Grace, I cannot achieve anything.' When the task is completed, let us not forget to thank Him for His help and support.

Above all, let us ask this of the Lord that we may always think of Him and be blessed by His all-encompassing Grace.

Words of Wisdom

You have to work at it, like everything else. It's easy to put God on the back burner or to turn to Him only when you have a problem. A lot of people use prayer when they are in need, then stop. To have a strong relationship with God, you have to keep going back to it. Like an athlete has to work hard to improve his skills, you have to maintain your faith to strengthen it.

—John Braham

Certain thoughts are prayers. There are moments when, whatever be the attitude of the body, the soul is on its knees.

—Victor Hugo

Remember this. When people choose to withdraw far from a fire, the fire continues to give warmth, but they grow cold. When people choose to withdraw far from light, the light continues to be bright in itself, but they are in darkness. This is also the case when people withdraw from God.

—*St Augustine*

Lesson 30

THE SECRET

Think positively. Eat sparingly. Exercise regularly. Walk as much as you can. Be careful to see that your thoughts and actions are clean. A guilty mind breeds many diseases. Herein, lies the secret of a happy, healthy and harmonious life.

A young lady returns home after a tough day at the office. She is mentally and physically exhausted. Her back is aching; her head is splitting; she can't face food. All she wants to do is take a hot bath and collapse on her bed.

Then the phone rings. It is from her best friend who has just come back after a holiday abroad. The friend wants to meet her and take her out to a five-star hotel for a special dinner party. And she's got such exciting gifts that she wants to hand over as soon as possible. Can she please come over?

The girl is galvanised into action. In a jiffy, she is ready—bathed, spruced, dressed, made-up, perfumed and looking like million dollars! She tears out of the house to catch up with her friend and spends an exciting evening; she returns home late at night, loaded with presents, which she opens and admires, not once but several times. And when she goes to bed, she can't sleep for sheer excitement!

It is all in the mind!

Everything changes when your attitude changes. Your attitudes control your body. When the girl's attitude was negative, her mind signalled weariness and exhaustion to the body, 'I'm tired! I'm tired!' The body responded to the message with sluggishness. It began to believe that it needed to collapse, it could not carry on! Her entire metabolism slowed down, accepting the message of the mind.

The phone call changed all that. Her mind now burst with enthusiasm and excitement. She was ready to go out, meet her friend, catch up with all the news and share a lovely meal with her; she had to get ready! Her emotions were now calling a different tune. 'Hurry, Hurry!' She picked up strength, energy, vitality and a spark. She was ready for anything now!

It is a clinically-proven fact that your body reacts to your attitude. I know bankers and financiers who suffered a heart attack when their investments proved to be bad. Equally, I have known chronically ill patients revive miraculously when a marriage is announced or a baby is born in the family. Bad news can make you ill, and good news can make you well. Negative emotions create an imbalance in your body, leading to ill-health; positive emotions restore the balance, bringing good health. Your body reacts to your attitude and changes your state of health. If you wish to change your life, you only have to change your attitude.

Understanding

How can you develop the spirit of optimism? Let me offer you a few practical suggestions: Believe in yourself—believe and achieve! When you believe in yourself and work hard, God blesses your efforts. You become a colleague of God.

Do only that which you feel is right and true. Nothing in life brings about unhappiness and failure more surely than lack of honesty and integrity.

Always do your best. When you give the world the best that you are capable of, the best will come back to you!

Have full faith and trust in the Divine Wisdom that designs and orders the scheme of things. Realise that mercy underlines all that happens to you.

Fix a goal and work towards it. Realise that you are unique, and that God made you for a special purpose. Discover that special purpose and make it your goal.

Always be positive in your approach and attitude to life. Do not focus your attention on problems and difficulties. Remember, there is no problem that does not have a solution.

Plan for each day of your life. Everyday, when you get up in the morning, you must plan on what you wish to do that day. Don't forget that time is the most precious of all commodities, and you cannot afford to waste even a moment! As Benjamin Franklin put it, 'If we take care of the minutes, the years will take care of themselves.'

Enthusiasm can work wonders. No matter what tasks you have at hand, do them with enthusiasm. If you wish to succeed at anything, you have to be enthusiastic about it.

Never, never, never give up! Whenever you have set a goal before you, whenever you set out to accomplish something, never, never, never give up! Difficulties may arise; obstacles may impede your progress; you may fail again and again. But let your failures become stepping stones to success, not stopping stones!

And finally, contact the source of all success and prosperity—God. He is the storehouse of abundance and prosperity. Learn to contact Him personally. Never miss out on your daily appointment with God.

Let us learn to rely more and more on God. The Divine invites us to surrender ourselves to Him, and offer all our efforts to Him in the spirit of dedication as Krishna *Arpanam.* He invites us to hand our problems over to Him.

Do you have a better option than the best?

Warming Up

Today's task is very simple: Eat well; pray well; take adequate exercise; think positively and keep your heart clean!

Words of Wisdom

It is our own mental attitude which makes the world what it is for us. Our thoughts make things beautiful; our thoughts make things ugly. The whole world is in our own minds.

—*Swami Vivekananda*

Our attitudes control our lives. Attitudes are a secret power working twenty-four hours a day, for good or bad. It is of paramount importance that we know how to harness and control this great force.

—*Tom Blandi*

A great attitude does much more than turn on the lights in our worlds; it seems to magically connect us to all sorts of serendipitous opportunities that were somehow absent before the change.

—*Earl Nightingale*

The greatest discovery of my generation is that human beings can alter their lives by altering their attitudes of mind.

—*William James*

Lesson 31

RELIGION IS LIFE

I have met many who will go to any length to prove the superiority of their religion over those of others.

They will hold endless discussions and debates. They will even fight for it, and die for it.

But I have met very few who live for their religion—who bear witness to the great teaching in deeds of daily living.

Religion is life!

The following 'true stories' have been widely reported on the internet in recent times:

There is a small village called Payakaraopeta in Andhra Pradesh. It is like a million other villages in the country. It has its own temple atop a small hillock. The pujari in this temple dedicated to the Goddess Durga is like any other pujari you will find in a small Indian village. The only thing that sets him apart is his name: Sheikh Mira Sahib.

Everyday, the devout people of the village climb the unpaved steps of Seethamma Hill to pray to the Goddess. On Tuesdays and Fridays, the people from surrounding villages congregate at the temple. Mira Sahib guides them all in performing various poojas. All the devotees treat him with love and respect and gratefully acknowledge him as their temple priest. With a shaven head, bare-chested and wearing a dhoti, Mira Sahib begins his day at the temple at seven, and till late afternoon stays busy praying or helping the pilgrims.

He then returns home to attend to his chores. The temple is built and maintained by the villagers, and Mira Sahib receives no salary from the Religious Endowments Board of the state government. His earning is the *dakshina* willingly given to him by the devotees. He is happy, and they are very happy with him.

The other 'story' is of Dawood Khan, who has made it his life's mission to study North India's most beloved scripture, *Shri Ram Charita Manas* by Tulsidas. Not only is he an expert on this sacred text, he actually goes from village to village, giving discourses to the people on the scripture, and simultaneously spreading the message of communal harmony across Raipur, in his own small way, one step at a time.

To quote him:

> My teacher inspired me to appear for the *Ram Charita Manas* examination and I was declared the winner, attaining marks of first division. Since then, I have been preaching *Ram Charita Manas*. Many orthodox people protest, but I tell them that this is what I have been doing and this is what I will continue to do.

For both Mira Sahib and Dawood, service to mankind is the best religion one can practise! Issues of superiority and insistence on one true faith are alien to these men, who believe in fulfilling duties of daily life in the true spirit of the Gita, which maintains that the Lord is there to receive us, no matter which path we choose to follow, in order to reach Him!

Understanding

All paths lead us to God. Therefore, fights, arguments, discussions, debates and differences in the name of the religion are futile. You can follow the path that draws you; let another follow the path that draws him; yet another can take the path he believes is the best for him. Ultimately, all of you will arrive at the same destination.

A man came to Sadhu Vaswani and said, 'You say God is love; God is mercy. Why is it that your God stands by and watches while there is so much violence and suffering in the world?'

Sadhu Vaswani pointed to a tablecloth, which he had just removed for wash. At the back of the cloth was a mishmash of crisscrossed stitches, with knots and ties and tangles. It all looked so untidy. But when the cloth was turned right side up, the man saw on it, beautifully embroidered, the words: God is love. 'It is we who turn religion inside out,' the master explained. 'God is love; God is mercy, when we see life right.'

Sadhu Vaswani, constantly urged us, 'Let us talk of religion less, practise more!' We need to follow his wise counsel now, more than ever.

We need to put into practice the great truths and ideals of religion in our daily lives. And if we really take the trouble to study the great religions of the world, we will learn that they too stress on the ideals of love, peace, service, piety, prayer and brotherhood.

I humbly submit to you, that rivalry in religion is meaningless. There can be no rivalry among true religions. If such rivalry has become rampant today, it is due to want of knowledge and lack of reverence.

Warming Up

Today, reflect on this beautiful sloka, which you will find in Chapter IV of the Bhagavad Gita:

> However men approach Me, even so do I greet them; for the path men take from every side is Mine, O Arjuna!

Speaking to his dear devoted disciple Arjuna, the Lord says, 'At the end of each path do I stand. All ways are My ways. All men everywhere walk to Me!'

Sadhu Vaswani's comments on this sloka are truly memorable:

His path, indeed, is the one path; there is no other. He is the One Bridge that spans the sea of sorrow, the Bridge of Light. The Bridge has diverse colours, and each is called by a different name. The Bridge has different sections or stages. *Jnana*, bhakti, karma are some of the names used by men to indicate what helps them to cross, but the path for all is still His path.

Words of Wisdom

As the different streams having their sources in different places, all mingle their water in the sea, so, O Lord, the different paths which men take through different tendencies, various though they appear, crooked or straight, all lead to Thee.

—*Swami Vivekananda*

Whosoever comes to Me, though whatsoever form, I reach him; all men are struggling through paths which in the end lead to Me.

—*Srimad Bhagavad Gita*

God can be realised through all paths. All religions are true. The important thing is to reach the roof. You can reach it by stone stairs or by wooden stairs or by bamboo steps or by a rope. You can also climb up by a bamboo pole.

—*Sri Ramakrishna*